Beyond the Silence
Listening for Democracy

Edited by J. Cynthia McDermott

HEINEMANN
Portsmouth, NH

Heinemann
A division of Reed Elsevier Inc.
361 Hanover Street
Portsmouth, NH 03801–3912
http://www.heinemann.com

Offices and agents throughout the world

© 1999 by Heinemann

The editor and publisher wish to thank those who have generously given permission to reprint borrowed material:

"Offering Challenges, Creating Cognitive Dissonance" by Alfie Kohn. From *The Active Learner: A Foxfire Journal for Teachers,* ed. Sara Day Hatton. Published by The Foxfire Fund, Inc., Mountain City. Copyright © 1997 by The Foxfire Fund, Inc. Reprinted by permission. For reprints or subscriptions, contact The Foxfire Fund, Inc.; P.O. Box 541; Mountain City, GA 30562–0541.

An earlier version of "The Real Ropes Course: The Development of Social Consciousness" by Shelley Berman was published in the *ESR Journal,* February 1989.

On the cover: Dorothea Lange, "A Salute of Innocence," courtesy of the Library of Congress, Prints & Photographs Division, FSA-OWI Collection.

LA 217. 2 B49 1999
Library of Congress Cataloging-in-Publication Data
Beyond the silence : listening for democracy / edited by J. Cynthia
  McDermott.
        p.   cm.
    Includes bibliographical references and index.
    ISBN 0-325-00072-7
    1. Education—Aims and objectives—United States—Case studies.
  2. Education—Social aspects—United States—Case studies.
  3. Democracy—Study and teaching—United States—Case studies.
  4. School improvement programs—United States—Case studies.
  5. Curriculum change—United States—Case studies. I. McDermott,
  J. Cynthia.
  LA217.2B49 1999
  370'.973—dc21   98-30141
                                                                    CIP

Editor: Lois Bridges
Production: Vicki Kasabian
Cover design: Darci Mehall/Aureo Design
Cover photo: Dorothea Lange, "A Salute of Innocence"
Manufacturing: Louise Richardson

Printed in the United States of America on acid-free paper
02 01 00 99 98   ML   1 2 3 4 5

To my children, Jason and Dana,
for teaching me the power of democracy
and to Jeff for his untiring support

Contents

8 Social Responsibility and Learning for Life

Foreword

What an exhilarating time to be an educator! I believe our democracy is now taking its first wobbly steps in a profound historical transition, and whether we learn to walk this new path with grace depends in large measure on the creativity and courage of our teachers.

In a nutshell, I've come to see that the definition of democracy I grew up with—democracy as a distant structure of government (what's done for us and to us!)—just can't work. Our problems are simply too deep, too complex, too interrelated to be solved from the top down. Solutions require the experience, insight, and ingenuity of those most directly affected. Now, on the surface this doesn't sound too controversial. But in fact it suggests nothing less than redefining democracy itself. And this means that we must find the courage (and enjoy the fun as well!) to challenge deeply embedded myths about the nature of democratic public life, the necessary contribution of citizens, and even the meaning of the good life itself.

Take the nature of public life. In millions of subtle and not-so-subtle messages, our culture bombards us with debilitating messages denying our role in shaping our own future. For example:

Public life is what someone else—a celebrity or big shot—has.

If I'm not a celebrity, public life is unappealing and unrewarding. It's all ugly conflict.

Public life competes with—even detracts from—a satisfying private life, and that's where the real rewards of life are.

My only job as a citizen is to vote. Then I can sit back and blame the corrupt and the incompetent.

Since all we citizens do is vote and assign blame, public life requires no special learning.

If each of these myths is an obstacle to creating a truly functional democracy—one that works because it is inclusive, accountable, and built on the values, interests, and insights of its citizens—then what's to be done?

Fortunately, millions of Americans are asking that question—and in their answers they are seeding the emergence of a new culture of democracy. In it, democracy is not something we have but what we do, a way of life that involves us daily—not just at the ballot box but in the classroom, community, workplace, service agency, as well as in relation to media and government.

Certainly the emergence of this new, more effective culture of democracy is not possible without the leadership of educators. It is in the classroom that we learn lessons that either prepare us for satisfying, rewarding roles in cocreating a common future, or reinforce feelings of powerlessness.

In other words, no one is born a citizen, no matter what legal rights we think we hold. Citizenship in a democracy is a learned art, one that our culture has yet to take seriously. The teachers in *Beyond the Silence: Listening for Democracy* understand this truth in their bones. They understand that democracy, meaning a culture of common responsibility, must be taught. It must be taught as a daily, satisfying practice. As they teach the arts of democracy—decision making, active listening, negotiation, mediation, evaluation, and creative conflict resolution— educators are making possible the emergence of a culture of democracy that rises to the enormous challenges of the twenty-first century.

That sounds weighty and somber indeed. But I love this book because it doesn't preach. Instead it takes the reader right into the classroom experience of democratic experimentation. With a plethora of examples, admissions of missteps, humility, and heart, it simply convinces the reader to find the courage to give it a try.

And courage it takes. For, as this book makes clear, educating for democracy by definition can't be taught by instruction, neat guidelines, simple dos and don'ts. Like any art, its practice is unique to the artist and must be a genuine creation of the artist. Fortunately, you'll find plenty of evidence from the exuberance in the voices in this book that the rewards are plenty worth the effort.

From my observations, once youngsters learn the arts of democracy and the associated habits of mind and heart, that genie will never go back in the bottle. The children in these stories are enriched forever as they learn that their voices count—that they can act effectively on their values in the larger world.

At the same time, these children, with their teachers' guidance, are learning they've been sold a bill of goods about what will bring satisfaction in their lives. Our society tells us that the rewards of living are primarily in our private worlds—limited to our intimate relationships and the accumulation of wealth. But these teachers and students are countering that false notion. Even in the face of unremitting media messages to the contrary, women in a recent survey placed making a difference in the world (64 percent) ahead of financial success (50 percent) and rewarding career (51 percent). Men ranked making a difference high as well. And psychologists now report that the happiest and healthiest among us are those who are involved in their communities and have a purpose in life larger than themselves. In essence, the educators in this book are helping our society grasp a constructive response to what could be a frightening realization—that our society's inherited notion of democracy as a static structure has failed. Breaking new ground, leaving behind failed cultural paradigms, takes nerve—nerve that is fed by hope. And where do we get hope? From each other, of course. That is why I am delighted that Cynthia McDermott has put together such an engaging book. The antidote to the failed notion of democracy as what somebody else does is the generation of a new culture of democracy as the living practice of citizens. There is no more important work in our nation today than that of educators such as those you'll meet between these covers—those nurturing, skilled, courageous citizens.

Frances Moore Lappé

Frances Moore Lappé is the author of Diet for a Small Planet *and co-director of the Center for Living Democracy.*

Acknowledgments

There are many folks to thank for making this book possible. A special thanks to Hilton Smith for his spirit and for making it possible for me to get to know Cliff and Terry and their important work. Thanks to JoAnne Ishimine who has taught me how to stay sane, Alfie Kohn for saying what I believe, Shelley Berman for my first adventure on a ropes course, and Dave Nettell who informs my work. A nod to those on whose shoulders I stand: Dewey, Addams, Gordon, Glasser, Kohl, and Freire.

A special thanks to my colleagues Lois Bridges, Sharon Setoguchi, Kate Thomas, Frances Moore Lappé, Peter McLaren, and all of the other contributors to this book, particularly the children: Oscar Castillo, Carla Gentle, Nicole Windover, Christopher Tafolla, Kristine Lozano, Naki May, Carlos Lopez, Ricardo Ramirez, Brenda Solorio, Rachel Mejia, Cathy Millan, Keiko Iida, Joanna Poceta, Janaki Jugannath, Taylor Eaton, Sierra French, Ryan Morris, Zachary Kutlow, Jerico Musngi, Audrey Rodarte-Griffith, Michael Brown, Mark Griego, Andrew Alonzo, Aide Herrera, Amanda Werth, Amy Chavez, Antonio Pessegueiro, Jeff Kerby, Caleb Engel, Beth Moody, Harvey Brimbuela, Krystal Toure, David Cordero, Ascot Tabucan, Edgar Morales, Mayra Moran, Cristina Herrera, Ruzelle Nocon, Richard Raquel, Zer Reyes, Claudia Luna, Abe Baquir, Laurie Virtusio, and Carlos Cortez.

Introduction

The purpose of this book is to encourage educators to create democratic classrooms. But what is a democratic classroom? It is a place where all of the participants—students, teachers, and paraprofessionals—have a voice in the decisions that are made. It is not a place of chaos, where each individual does what they want. Nor is it a place where external authoritarian decisions dictate and govern classroom life. It is, however, an environment where deliberate, conscious, caring, and ethical decisions are made for the well-being of everyone. A democratic classroom is alive with the singular possibility that everyone can learn and be successful but never at the expense of anyone else.

This possibility unfortunately eludes too many of our students. Schools today continue to teach much the same way they did a hundred years ago. In the introduction to *The Struggle to Continue,* Patrick Shannon (1990) describes a literacy lesson; although it reads as though it were written today, the observations are field notes from 1883. Many of us learned in that industrially based system, which taught us to follow directions, to be punctual, and to never question authority. But is that enough? Beyond the content, we learned lessons that have not always stood us in good stead. I learned that the fastest student was the smartest, that doing what I was told was the best choice, that making my work look great would get me a better grade, and that my loyalty to friends was contingent upon how it helped me in school. I learned to be silent and let others speak for me.

Students tell me that things have not changed. Students—disinterested, difficult, and bored students who are bright and creative and funny and confused—have told me that school is stupid, that nobody cares about them or what they think, and that nobody listens. These are not students heading for Harvard. Some of them may never earn a high school diploma. But they are our future, and in order to engage them and encourage them to be "educated" we must begin to use practices that will change the goals and objectives of public education. The latest instructional strategy, a packaged program, or national or local standards will do little to convince our children that we care and that they should engage in learning the way school defines it. Because we often do not know how to "help" students who are disinterested, we provide them with opportunities to fail.

1

The price society pays for their failure is high; the price to the individual higher still. And yet we continue using a "teacher-dominates" banking model where we teachers, the experts, deposit information, dole out directions and advice, and ask them to respond on our terms. This model encourages passivity, resentment, and poor quality work. As important, it also fails to encourage the necessary citizenship skills critical to democratic living.

I have tried to learn and develop these skills on my own outside of school because they make me a more valuable citizen and a "good neighbor." I've had to learn ways to pose problems and then solve them. Sometimes I've had to solve them with other people and needed to learn how to listen. Sometimes I've been asked what I want as part of the solution and I have not known how to figure that out. Getting along, working together, thinking critically, engaging my passion, using my time wisely, being an active citizen who votes, reads, recycles, and generally understands my interconnectiveness to the world are skills and activities I want to enlarge and challenge the public school community to enhance in children. This is what democratic teaching can do and that is why I asked friends, colleagues, students, and practitioners to create this democratic primer with me. As I have practiced the skills in this book, I have become convinced that students can learn them best in democratic classrooms. This book addresses how to do it.

First Things First

What do you need to know and learn to get started? What should you do first? There is no easy answer but what helped me was replacing my practice of behaviorism. This psychological model of external control is antithetical to democracy. It is a belief that you the teacher can make a student do something that you want. You can turn a card, place a marble in a jar, write a name on the board, send letters home, or offer ice cream parties or praise. Or you can give a dirty look, tell a child his work is poor, punish a child with lowered grades, not listen, and so on. I could fill a book with all the ways I've seen teachers try to make students do what they want because the teachers feel it's good for them and will best serve the students in the long run.

There are students who will conform to this process, but it sends powerful messages: that the work is not important, that students must be forced to do it, and that others are the experts. Students learn many messages about who they are and what is important with this psychological model but not perhaps what we would like them to learn. When students worry more about doing poorly, not following the rules, and being perceived as failures, trust disappears.

Second, creating a trusting environment is central to a democratic classroom. Why? Because if the skills we want for students include telling the truth, discovering for themselves what they want, speaking up, and solving problems, no one will speak the truth if they are not trusted. Creating a sense of community requires team building, active listening, and problem posing and solving.

Third, independent thinking is essential and can be encouraged through reflection and self-evaluation. As a democratic classroom of learners begins to coalesce and develop, the process is not always smooth. As you begin your journey, you and your democratic shareholders will encounter disagreements, problems, and difficult challenges. In order to solve them, all of us need skills to listen to each other, identify the problems, and create opportunities to try solutions and treat each other with respect. These skills can be learned and practiced by any group and are necessary for the success of a democratic classroom.

The fourth piece is the curriculum. What do you want the children to know? What does the district want children to know? What are they interested in learning? What do you enjoy teaching? As you answer these questions, you and the students can then decide what the "givens" will be and how they will be learned. A democratic classroom is a place where the curriculum is covered but in agreement with all of the shareholders.

What Gets in the Way

There are, unfortunately, elements that interfere with the democratic process. First, some students may be reluctant to make decisions and take responsibility, and so the process bogs down. Time and practice will move it along. Second, staff members may question what you are doing or ask you to not rock the boat. Sometimes students come to enjoy the opportunity for choice so much that they may even pressure other adults to try it out. Third, because democratic classrooms attend to tasks often ignored in other classrooms, you and your students may explore the curriculum more slowly. But since students will be engaged in what matters to them and will learn more, they will be successful. There may be other difficulties but not more so than any other classroom. Actually, as students feel ownership of the class and the curriculum, many of the usual problems with management and quality of work begin to disappear.

How to Read This Book

As I began to write, I tried to separate the pieces that create the democratic classroom, but it was difficult. A democratic classroom is holistic.

You can't create team building without problem solving, for example. So I began with experts whose work had informed my practice. I then asked democratic classroom teachers and their students to respond to the experts' work. Accordingly, you'll notice that each chapter is divided into multiple sections featuring the work of an expert and then one or two responses from practitioners and students whose classroom work is informed by that expert. It is exciting to share the voices of such a diverse group—from well-seasoned practitioners, to new teachers, and from first graders through senior high school students. Their voices represent the diversity of developing democratic classrooms.

In a democracy, the intention is to hear all of the voices. Unfortunately we often do not hear the voices of our students or teachers. If you have been silenced and know that the same is true for your students, you might decide to try the ideas in this book. You can read what teacher educators say as well as the teachers with whom they work. More important, you can read the voices of the children—the true experts on the life on the classroom. Give the book to your students and see what they think. Perhaps they are as hopeful about the promise of democracy as the children from 1942 shown on the cover of this book.

In a poem entitled "Action," Denise Levertov ends with this line: "Little by little one comes to know / the limits and depths of power." This book is about shared power and we invite you to give it a try.

Works Cited

Levertov, D. 1979. *Collected Earlier Poems 1940–1960*. New York: New Directions.

Shannon, P. 1990. *The Struggle to Continue: Progressive Reading Instruction in the United States*. Portsmouth, NH: Heinemann.

1

Teacher Trust, Student Control, and Shared Power

Our Invitation

This chapter peeks into the life of two elementary classrooms where children are encouraged to choose caring behavior. Joanne Trupp, Jessica Fairbanks, and their students reflect on how this change in psychology has affected their work. Alfie Kohn's interview discusses the need to create caring classrooms where students make decisions about behavior and curriculum. He also discusses the need to move beyond the behaviorist processes of rewards and punishments so that students have the opportunity to learn self-control and responsibility.

Offering Challenges,
Creating Cognitive Dissonance

Alfie Kohn

Alfie, a former teacher turned author, writes and speaks widely
on human behavior, education, and social theory.

Q: *When did you become aware of the need for student choice, and*
what are some of the ways you involved your students in your classes?

A: I became aware of most of what students need after I taught,
I'm sorry to report. I did several things that in retrospect gave me some
source of satisfaction or pride but a lot more that make me wince when
I look back on how little I knew about what teachers ought to do. I
brought students in, for the most part, in a peripheral way in deciding
how they would respond to an essay question or to pick from a range
of questions when it was time for assessment; because that was all I
knew; it was all that I had experienced from elementary school to graduate school. I missed the point about how important it is for kids to
have substantial amounts of discretion in figuring out what they're
going to learn and how and why. I came to that belatedly from watching teachers who were much better than I was, reading research and
other people's views from Dewey to the present day, and thinking
about it a lot. Were I to go back in the classroom today, I would certainly do things differently.

Q: *In witnessing other teachers, did you observe obstacles they*
encountered, and can you tell us how they dealt with them?

A: One major impediment to giving students choice is the
teacher's own reservations about it. There's no magic solution for
someone who isn't sure this is going to work except to be in a community of adults who can talk together at regular intervals about what
they're doing and to complain and to search for solutions together and
to visit each other's classrooms. I think some of the best teachers are
those who are lucky enough to be in the best schools and are able to do
that. Another obstacle is that the students themselves are unaccus-
tomed to freedom and react at least at first by engaging in more kinds
of behavior, good and bad, than ever before because the controls have
finally been loosened. They're able to exercise their autonomy for the
first time and that's messy and noisy and aggravating. The teachers I've
talked to always suggest patience and also bringing the students in on
this very problem. Then if for example students make ridiculous
choices or sit there paralyzed, unable to do anything except to say
"You're the teacher; this is your job," the great teachers are able to
react without resentment and too much confusion. They say, "What a

great topic for discussion! What's my job? How do you feel when someone tells you what to do all day? Will you say you're too young to make decisions?" Or if students are sitting there passively during class, that opens all kinds of possibilities providing the teacher can figure out why this is happening. Is it because they don't feel safe in this classroom? If so, how can *we*—underscore *we*—change this situation so that nobody is afraid of being left out? If students are sitting there quietly because they have nothing to say at the moment, then forcing them to speak up is worse than doing nothing. If they're merely shy by temperament, that leads you to react in a very different way than if they don't feel their comments are going to be taken seriously.

I think most teachers who have tried to give students choices have realized that the worst of all possible courses is to ask their opinion and then dismiss it. For example, by saying they haven't made a responsible choice, which means they haven't done what the teacher wanted and that therefore their decision doesn't count, they feel used and therefore are unlikely to make that mistake again.

I always advise teachers to start out easily with a decision or a question that is circumscribed and the results of which they can live with until they are able to fashion with the students a classroom that's more democratic.

I made a few efforts along those lines when I was teaching. I gave them the chance to write in journals back before that was fashionable. I'm not sure if it was the dimension of choice to make the decision about what to write or what made that such a good decision. It opened up a new world to me of the students' inner lives. I went from looking at the surface of the ocean to becoming Jacques Cousteau, explorer of the deep, where even students who had never come up to talk to me and who would not feel safe talking in front of their peers about the things that gripped their inner lives were opening up to me. If only because it created a kind of relationship under the surface or alongside our public life in the classroom, it was a valuable decision, and the only restraint I put on the journals was that they be something more than a dry chronicle of events. They had to talk about how they thought or felt about what was going on and of course I promised them confidentiality, and that stuff was far richer and more meaningful to them than almost anything I was doing in the regular curriculum.

Q: *Did you encounter obstacles?*

A: With the journals, no, primarily not. But I wish I had done more along those lines so that I could have had to work through obstacles I know good teachers do every day. It took me some years to figure this out, but I had the idea when I was teaching high school that a course was something a teacher developed on his or her own, built in a garage and polished like an automobile, and took pride in, as I did in one course that I taught for many years on existentialism. I honed that reading list, I carefully constructed the balance of activities in the class, and the papers to assign and the reading. Then I took it out of the garage when it was time to teach and brought it out to the students. It took me many years to figure out that as good a course as that was or as exciting a reading list that it had, I didn't understand the first thing about teaching because it made approximately as much sense to think of a course that way as it would for a single person to say that "I have this great marriage waiting—I can't wait to meet somebody to be my husband or wife and take part in it with me."

It was based on a fallacious view of learning. There is no course until the students and you create it together, and I didn't see that when I was teaching. When you get right down to it, either you believe the course is fully formed and delivered to the students or you realize there is nothing but a framework and hunches and first starts and the course itself is created together. I think I see it now but I didn't then. It's not just a matter of how much choice about what books they're going to read; it is a matter of a philosophy of teaching. So a lot of the bumps and barriers and obstacles that great teachers encounter, I, like the great majority of teachers, never had to contend with because I was not teaching authentically to begin with. That's a hard thing for me to admit, and I can only say I wish I had seen it sooner.

Q: *As teachers we really struggle with how we can help students learn to make good choices. Have you struggled with that, and what is your thinking on it?*

A: Well, the first step in making a good choice is to *have* a choice rather than being told what to do most of the time. Kids learn to make good decisions by making decisions. If we want our kids to take responsibility for their behavior, then we have to give them responsibilities along with guidance and support and love. But they also have to be making decisions that matter. I often hear teachers talk about how they give kids the chance to choose when the teachers don't really care about the outcome, and of course that's nothing close to a democratic classroom. The kids have to be able to make decisions when it matters very much to the teacher because that's authentic choice. There are examples all over the place of what I call pseudochoice where they have to make the so-called right decision or it doesn't count or it's these awful attempts to coerce kids that are wrapped in the language of choice, such as "Would you like to finish your homework now or do it after school?" This is not a choice at all of course. It's saying to the kid "Do what I tell you or I'll punish you," and this is a staple of many disciplinary programs. We help kids make good choices by making sure they are informed about the options they have and also that the options are appealing. A kid who gets to choose between two workbooks or silly essay questions or the time of day in which to memorize math facts is not being offered real choice. Somewhere Shakespeare says there is little choice in rotten apples.

Q: *Have you talked to teachers who are struggling with this with positive results?*

A: Yes, absolutely. That's where I've learned most of what's going on in my thinking. It's the practical realities in classrooms around the country that I've witnessed that animate my work and inform it. When I walk into a second-grade classroom in St. Louis and watch the kids running their own class meetings to solve problems that have come up, where one child is the facilitator and another is the recorder, thus teaching language skills, and the teacher is just sprawled out on the floor with the rest of them as they maintain a discipline, a patience, and a respect that would have blown me away if they were seventeen but they were in fact seven years old. Or the story of a teacher in California who came back from her break to find the kids already huddled together excitedly talking about something, even though recess wasn't over, and when she asked what was going on was told a problem had happened during recess and they were holding a meeting to fix it themselves. The kids didn't get there right away. In both these examples and many others I could share, what I'm really looking at is the hard work of the teacher in helping them to become empowered, to take responsibility not only for their own behavior but for the actions and values and feelings of everyone else as well as learning the skills of how to make decisions together.

For heaven's sake, most books and classes to which teachers are exposed take it for granted that the teacher must be in control of the classroom, and the only question is how you get and keep that control most effectively. What I want to call into question is the idea that the teacher ought to be in unilateral control of what's going on. I didn't question that premise when I was teaching. I never saw a classroom where a group of learners democratically figured out what the course ought to be, what to learn, how to learn, why to learn, how to treat each other, how they wanted to solve problems. I'd never read about or seen it, so my classroom reflected my own experience. I imagine that's true for millions of teachers around the country. It's all the more remarkable, then, when you come across an example of somebody who miraculously has figured out that kids have to be active learners and that the best teaching is not where the teacher is most firmly in charge.

Q: *Looking at the concept of rewards, when you were teaching were you deeply entrenched in the concept of rewards? How did you* *move away from giving rewards, and what obstacles did you encounter?*

A: I was never in a situation where I was expected to give out gold stars and stickers and the like so for me as a teacher the discouraging effect of extrinsic motivators was embodied primarily in grades. One of the few things I figured out on my own was that I had to do everything possible to neutralize the destructive effects of these things that I was required to give. I was teaching at a school of kids who had been prepared to get into Harvard since their earliest days, a process I have come to call Preparation H, and these were kids for whom the absence of grades created what I can only call existential vertigo. I told the kids that I had to give them grades at the end although I didn't like it and then I told them why I didn't like it. Today what I hope I would do is bring them in on the discussion of the effects of grades and how it has led them in their past to do only what is required and to pick the easiest possible assignments so as to maximize the probability of getting an A and so on. I didn't figure that out back then. What I've since learned is that the best teachers do a lot more asking than telling. But at least I figured out that the grades themselves were destructive and I said to them, "I have to give you a grade at the end of the term, but I cannot in good conscience ever put a letter or a number on anything you do, and I won't. All I will do when time permits is write a comment and/or talk to you about what you've done." Now that could have backfired easily if I'd left it at that because some of them would have been led to think even more about their grades because now I was keeping their grades a secret from them, and that would have been counterproductive in the extreme. So I told them that if they really needed to know what grade this paper would get or what grade they would get if one were given at this point in the term, they could come up and see me and we would talk together. I'm pleased to report that as time went on, fewer students felt the need to do that because when I stopped pushing these grades into their faces by writing one on a paper they had written for me, they began to be more engaged with the subject matter. And at some point I had to give them a grade, but I wasn't going to make it any more salient than I had to, and that's a piece of advice I give to teachers now. Until we're able to work together to eliminate traditional letter grades, which I believe are inimical to real learning, we need to do everything we can in our own classrooms to make them invisible.

A lot of the problem in the practices of teachers and the practice to which teachers themselves are subjected is the function of a very simple error, which is thinking of motivation as a single entity that one can have more or less of. We want kids to have more motivation and so we use rewards and punishments. We dangle goodies in front of them, but what psychologists have been telling us for decades is there are different kinds of motivation and they are not interchangeable. The most popular distinction is between intrinsic and extrinsic motivation, intrinsic being a fancy term for loving what it is you do and extrinsic motivation meaning that you do one thing in order that something else can happen such as that you achieve someone's approval or a dollar or an A or a pizza. But intrinsic and extrinsic aren't just different. Intrinsic is corrupted and attenuated by extrinsic motivation so that in general they tend to vary inversely—the more extrinsic, the less intrinsic, though that's not a hard-and-fast rule.

People simply try to motivate from the outside by saying, "Come on, folks, this is going to be on the test," or "I like the way Sara is sitting so nice and quiet and ready to work," or by giving out awards to a select group who have jumped through enough hoops, or by handing out stickers to kids who are well behaved or who have memorized their spelling words correctly. The people who are doing this don't think about extrinsic and intrinsic; they just think you can motivate kids, not realizing they are providing the kind of motivation that undermines what we really want to promote.

One of the reasons this persists in workplaces and classrooms and families is that we haven't understood that the question we need to ask is not "How motivated are my students?" That's a silly question. What we need to ask is *"How* are my students motivated?" In other words, what matters is not the amount but the type—and the traditional practices we use, again including praise, tend to be precisely the wrong kind of motivation that reduces what it is we really want kids to come away with, which is a commitment to decency and generosity and learning.

Q: *In* Punished by Rewards, *you say* "Praise is often a verbal reward used to control people." *It's such a struggle not to use praise. Do you find yourself struggling with it, and if so, how are you working to break that habit?*

A: Absolutely. Of all the things I teach about, this is probably the hardest for me to put in place in my own life because I have come to think of praise—I should say come to *do* praise— almost by second nature. It feels weird, chilly, sterile, as if you're withholding something when you don't slather on positive judgments. But I came to realize that I was praising more because I needed to say it than because the kid needed to hear it, and whenever that's true, boy, is it time to rethink our practices. So what you put in place of it is not sullen silence or criticism. To cast it that way is to create a false dichotomy. Rather what you want to do is to ask whether your judgment is really necessary and what its effects are likely to be. So, for example, instead of saying,

"Wow! That's terrific! You're really good at that!" I will talk less and ask more. "How did that feel? How were you able to come up with that solution? What's really exciting to you about this process—or boring? What are you going to work on next?" We want to offer kids and other adults encouragement and support and care and love, but that's very different from verbal doggie biscuits that often lead people to be praise junkies until it comes to the point of squeezing out the excitement about learning itself. We know tangible rewards can reduce kids' interest in whatever they had to do to get the reward. So can the relentless use of a powerful person's approval become the "goodie." And this becomes disempowering in the extreme.

I think about it all the time. I think about it with my young daughter; I think about it when I visit classrooms and offer feedback to teachers. I think about it when I myself am praised and reflect carefully on whether it's a good feeling or whether it's a way of someone else saying "I am arrogating to myself the power to decide if I liked your speech or your comment." You have to look very carefully both at your motive for praising as well as the effects it's having. If somebody says, "That's a nice tie," I don't take offense at that. But when a teacher says, "That's a very good story" or "I like the way you shared your sandwich," I think we have to be very careful about the intent behind such comments and the effect they're likely to have on the people who are most affected by them.

It's not a coincidence that the ugliest, most coercive discipline program I'm aware of, called Assertive Discipline, says that praise is the number one technique teachers should use. For teachers who recoil from a program as coercive as that one and yet have always assumed that positive reinforcement is terrific, there's an interesting challenge to be reconciled.

But even when our hearts are pure and we want to encourage kids rather than control them, we often miss the ways in which praise is likely to have the opposite effects. Sometimes when kids are praised, they act out even worse following the praise. Almost every elementary teacher has seen that, at least among some kids. And I think it's interesting to reflect on why that happens if praise is supposed to be so terrific. I think often what's going on is that the kids realize the most striking feature of a positive judgment is not that it's positive but that it is a judgment.

Q: *It's very difficult for teachers to explain why they use an approach to teaching that does not include rewards or contests. Do you know ways teachers have successfully explained their approach? What strategies would you give teachers who want to help parents and children and other teachers and administrators understand why they choose not to give rewards?*

A: Every time I give a speech or write an article or book on the topic, what I'm trying to do is help those teachers to make a case just by pointing out that we all want kids to be lifelong learners and that the use of extrinsic motivators makes that a little less likely. Let's look at awards. It's not merely the kids who lose who become demoralized and resentful and envious, it's the kids who win as well who are made to feel that their self-worth is contingent upon their continuing to triumph over other people. That's a recipe for neurosis if I ever heard one. Often people who oppose competition and extrinsic motivators are put on the defensive by a small number of tired arguments about how kids aren't all alike and some kids aren't motivated to do the work or how we want to recognize excellence. So I try to model responses teachers can use. For example, we can point out that genuine excellence comes from genuine encouragement, that over the long haul if we want kids to become both sharp thinkers and people who are in love with ideas, we can't choose the easy way out by trying to motivate them from the outside. I point out that the devices we use for that purpose tend to backfire. I recommend that teachers who are faced with administrators, colleagues, or parents who use the approaches that involve doing things *to* kids rather than working *with* them, start by talking about the goals they share for kids. Overwhelmingly, teachers and parents and administrators want the same thing. I start almost every workshop by asking people to reflect on their long-term goals for kids—what they would like kids to be like after they've left school—and I get the same words and phrases everywhere in the country, in urban schools and rural schools, and from elementary and secondary educators. Everybody talks about how we want kids to be curious and creative and filled with self-esteem and lifelong learners and responsible and all the rest of it. I recommend that teachers make use of those shared goals when they talk with others and then invite them to reflect on how the traditional techniques actually get in the way of helping kids reach the goals we all want them to reach.

Q: *In your work teaching teachers, what have you found to be successful in helping them to rethink the role of praise and rewards in teaching children?*

A: I use a combination of research results, real-life anecdotes, arguments, and jokes. I ask people to think about why techniques that we assume are desirable show up in programs that we detest. I ask people to think about why some people, some kids, tend to act out after we have praised them or why it is that some kids become less interested in being challenged after we've used these so-called motivators. I'm trying to create cognitive dissonance so they have to dig their way out from an apparent contradiction and eventually realize that the practices and premises they've relied on may be faulty.

Now, in addition to research studies, I have Oprah to add to this. I was on her show, and the producers decided to stage a replication of one of the experiments I describe in my book. They brought in a bunch of kids and told them that they were from a toy company and wanted these kids to evaluate a puzzle. Half of the kids were just asked to do it and the other half were paid five dollars for each puzzle they played with and then all of the kids individually were left alone in a room with a puzzle. And astonishingly, every kid who had not been paid continued playing with the puzzle on his or her own time, while nine out of ten kids who had gotten the reward wanted nothing to do with the puzzle after the experimenter had left. This is a remarkable, and I might add, widely broadcast confirmation of what dozens of studies have shown.

What I often do, which I hope is consistent with constructivist teaching, is to present examples of research results like that. There's one where kids who were rewarded with movie tickets or praise for drinking an unfamiliar beverage became a lot less interested in that beverage as compared to kids who were never rewarded in the first place. So I mention a result like that and then I say, you figure it out. What's going on here? Present the results to people and let them construct an account, a rationale for why this happened, and you don't have to hit them over the head with it. Teachers realize "if it's true for the puzzle or the beverage, maybe this is what I'm doing when I give out stickers. Maybe this is the effect I'm having unwittingly when I tell kids how much I love what they've produced. Maybe my kids' interest in learning is declining as a result of an emphasis on grades or scores." Then what we have to do is get the teachers together to figure out how to undo the damage and it becomes a question of implementation rather than a question of resistance to the merits of the argument. At least that's what I hope.

Q: *Is there anything you would like to say to our teacher readers about the work of teaching?*

A: When I conclude one of my own presentations, I try to leave teachers with two points. One is that if they have heard me say something that struck a nerve and made them extremely uncomfortable because I have indicted a practice they just engaged in that very morning, they might be tempted to wonder whether they are bad teachers. In fact, if they are even thinking in those terms, they are probably terrific teachers because they have the courage to think in those terms—that is, to be open to the possibility that they have done something not as well as it could have been done. The people I worry about are those who snort or smirk or sneer and dismiss the arguments and research as "unrealistic," which is the favorite adjective for dismissing something that is too threatening. The people who look stricken and gulp are the people whose classroom I want my kid in because they have the gumption to try to get better at what they do.

The other thought I might close with is that if someone is inclined to take a chance and do something different (not just adding some new techniques like getting kids on the Internet but really rethinking the whole philosophy of learning), they shouldn't try to do it alone. They should at the very least find a colleague to supply moral support and new ideas to help them avoid being burned out and depressed. For those who are bringing kids in on making decisions only to have the kids the very next year go back to workbooks and Assertive Discipline, it can be demoralizing. I always ask those teachers if there was a teacher when they were kids who made a difference in their life in just one year. I tell them they can be that teacher, but they can't be that teacher over a period of time unless they have found somebody to complain to and be inspired by. You know, we are interdependent creatures, like it or not. I think we might as well like it, own it, and recognize that we can both provide support and derive support from others even in an environment that isn't as welcoming as it ought to be.

Work Cited

Kohn, A. 1993. *Punished by Rewards: The Trouble with Gold Stars, Incentive Plans, A's, Praise, and Other Bribes.* Boston: Houghton Mifflin.

Trusting Students, Feeling Safe

Joanne Trupp and her first and second graders at Muir School, Long Beach Unified School District

Joanne teaches a multiage class and is in her third year of teaching.

I grew up in an era where I had little choice in what I wanted to learn at school or how that learning would occur, but somehow I knew that there had to be a more responsible, positive way for presenting children with the things they needed. As I progressed through the educational system, I also began to plan how I would build and nurture a classroom atmosphere if I was the teacher.

I began my journey by reading about the detrimental effects of extrinsic rewards. I began looking for a better way to reinforce students' understanding of a system not based on rewards. I had no idea how I was going to do this, just a sincere desire to become partners with my students in their own journey through education.

Then I was introduced to the writings of Alfie Kohn. Aha! Suddenly, I had a resource for the atmosphere that would become charged with the questions and directions of thirty young people poised to embark on the most exciting work of their lives.

From the very onset of the school year, the children and I discussed being partners in education. Students became immediately and directly involved in the social and physical environment and began making their own rules and subsequent consequences if those rules or norms were not followed. Believe me, they were harder on themselves than I would have ever been. At first, the rules were the typical ones: raise your hand to speak, do not get out of your seat without permission, keep your hands, feet, and body parts to yourself. They were the rules they knew from the previous school experience. The difficult part was eliminating rewards. I must admit their expectations of those remains an ongoing process that we must collaborate on each and every year. That first year, I succumbed to the schoolwide program of giving students prizes for finishing assigned work, but I soon discovered that some students produced work only when there was an object or privilege they wanted in return. If the particular prize wasn't of particular interest, their efforts essentially ceased. Some students practically gave up before they started. I was sinking fast out of frustration and so were they. This was a turning point; I realized that something had to change—and fast.

I knew of teachers who had class meetings and had actually seen one modeled during a teacher education course at the university, so I decided to give it a try. Our first meeting was really more me controlling the issues and the time, but it was a good opportunity to discuss with the students what was happening. It soon became obvious, how-ever, that they really didn't feel safe enough to take such a risk, voice their ideas, or express personal thoughts or concerns. From this shaky beginning our team meetings have evolved into a powerful collective voice for students that they freely share with each other and me, their teacher. They use a "talking stick" as a means for keeping order, and everyone has an opportunity to command their fellow students' full attention. (A talking stick is a device that is used to control dialogue. The class agrees that no one will speak unless they have the "talking stick." We have found that the most effective device is a koosh ball because it can be tossed from one child to another without fear of injury and students love to hold them.)

Our class meetings work like this: When they come in from recess, where there has been an altercation, they quickly arrange themselves into a circle on the rug. The decision for a meeting usually happens before the class enters the room so everyone knows the plan. Someone then takes the initiative to conduct a team meeting. They don't ask "permission," they know *they* are in control of the important decision making in their own classroom. These meetings have changed our team in very positive ways. Students are willing to take risks when they know they are in a safe environment. I modeled how to run these meet-ings, and students were invited to take my place. I can still call a meet-ing, but the students usually beat me to it. Meetings last from ten min-utes to an hour depending on the depth of the problem. Sometimes meetings are called to discuss the next steps in a project, so they are both affective and curricular in nature.

The other significant change was that students began making deci-sions that mattered. After that first shaky year, I was asked to become one of the teachers on our multiage team. I eagerly agreed and embarked on yet another new journey. I made one major change from the year before—I eliminated extrinsic rewards. It amazed me how quickly stu-dents become accustomed to rewards, even first and second graders. At the first team meeting, when the talking stick came my way, I mentioned that there would not be any special stickers, candy, or toys for producing work. That statement opened an interesting conversation as to why stu-dents thought they needed and required rewards. Talk revolved around what their responsibilities were and what mine were. We discussed what had happened the year before, and I asked them why students sometimes will only work for rewards. Their answers were revealing. They believed they couldn't work without them. They thought and believed they needed these little treats to do their work. I asked if they thought they could work without them and if they would be willing to give it a try. I stepped away from the circle and gave them time and space to discuss this dilemma. I was leaving the choice up to them.

They spent a long time discussing, laughing, arguing, and hashing out their opinions and ideas. Finally, someone came and retrieved me and told me they had come to a team decision. They had come to a consensus and decided to give it a try. That would be the turning point in our team. They liked the power to make decisions that mattered to them, and they also had learned to compromise in ways that were important to them personally and to the group as a whole. Their understanding of how to negotiate class-related issues has turned the fine art of debate into something every student in my classroom now feels passionate about. Each has learned to respect and appreciate differences, to give in gracefully when necessary, and to try to not let ridicule seep into their conversations. Group decision making has turned our classroom into a constantly changing environment where students make decisions throughout the day including how and when they do their work. Some students may choose to do a math choice while others are reading and I am guiding a group in a science lesson. This method has also given students the ultimate choice as to what they learn. Lessons evolve from their interest in a certain theme or idea. We discuss what they want to learn and how they would like to accomplish this.

We essentially create the curriculum as we go, beginning with what the district expects of us. I inform students about the district guidelines and what they are expected to know by the end of the year. From the list of "givens" we then embark on the decisions that involve the projects and activities that we do. We let our interests guide our decisions rather than what the next page of the textbook suggests. For some educators this would be maddening, but I have seen students interested in subjects that would seem far beyond their grasp. I have had students "surfing" the 'Net for research projects. I have had students directing lessons themselves and having the full attention, consideration, and respect of their peers that is normally awarded only to a teacher.

Here is an example of a project. The math curriculum requires that students know how to determine the area and perimeter. Students found this boring and unconnected, but one student generated a particular interest and challenged the class to design their own park. They figured out what they needed and designed it with a green belt and water and trees and Keep It Clean signs. We don't have parks like that around our neighborhood, and students knew that they could not really build one, but it was important for them to realize what a park might be like and to think about why their parks are not like the one they designed. They also got some real practice in perimeter and area as they looked at parks, measured them, and thought about how much room they wanted. Who knows; maybe next year they'll decide to build one!

All of us are taking risks, and I find the students' learning both accelerated and deepened. Recently, students were playing a math game called Addition Bingo and as they started, a fairly new student asked what he would get if he won. I was working in one corner of the class with a small group and as I listened I heard the tiniest voice say, "Knowledge." This was all that was needed for the game to continue; and it was a defining moment I will return to as I continue my journey in education. When I interviewed some of my students to add their voices to this book, here is what they told me.

> I feel safe in my class. When I am on the playground kids make fun of me, but when I go in the class I feel better because kids don't make fun of me. In the classroom, we don't sit in rows because we know how to sit anywhere we need to. We help each other. We have class meetings. We have a talking stick. Whoever has the talking stick talks. People talk only when they have the talking stick. The class meetings help people be nice. When kids do something wrong we don't scream at them. Sometimes we take care of the class because we know how to do those kind of things.
>
> Nicole Windover, Christopher Tafolla,
> and Kristine Lozano

> Last year I was in Mrs. Trupp's class. This year I went to third grade. My teacher does things different than Mrs. Trupp but that's OK because I learned how to make good choices and I use those choices this year. I know that I am the one in control of me, nobody else. I come everyday to help in Mrs. Trupp's class. I like that because the other students ask me for help and I can help them.
>
> Naki May

Naki at first had a hard time in a room where he had few choices. But as the first few weeks settled in, he found that coming to my room and helping the younger students gave him a chance to use the skills he had learned in our room. I believe that democratic classrooms can provide children with the ability to get to know themselves and figure out solutions on their own. That's what my students are doing and they are doing it well.

Giving Up Control

Jessica Fairbanks and her third and fourth graders at Billy Mitchell School, Lawndale School District, Lawndale, California

Jessica has taught for five years as a bilingual elementary educator.

Attempting to create a democratic classroom where student voices are heard and valued is an incredible daily struggle. I agree with Alfie Kohn that it can only be implemented in small steps and with loving patience. Each student is welcomed as part of a whole and recognized as a creative, valuable individual.

During one morning circle at the beginning of the year our second grade class addressed the issue of rules. My previous experiences with giving kids the control over rules and consequences usually led to jubilation, hurt feelings, and a true sense of chaos before a community of learners who cared about each other emerged.

My second grade class, however, rattled off a few standard rules with sweet, sensitive Oscar Castillo adding that maybe "we just shouldn't be allowed to move." That would surely keep everyone in line! I could hardly keep from busting up. The discussion faltered as we settled on everyone being nice to each other. Our consequences included warnings, time-out breaks away from group, and loss of recess time. Everyone agreed to tell the truth even if they might get in trouble. (No one really liked liars or tattletales.) The discussion took part of one afternoon and surprisingly never led to any bitterness or power struggle. We practiced what real apologies sounded like and talked about how our hearts felt when we make one or when we are waiting for one.

This discussion taught me that I had to make time for these important issues. Role playing and problem solving are central to how we relate to each other and value one another. Each day we begin with a community circle. We begin by welcoming each other as we sit in a circle. We practice greetings that are positive and affirming. "Good morning, Claudia, it's good to see you." Someone begins the circle and then each person introduced introduces the next person. We always conclude our morning circle with our "amigos handshake" as the students reach to their neighbors on each side and shake hands. We end with a friendly pat on the back.

This is my favorite part of the day for it sets the tone and shows the students that every voice counts. We use this circle to deal with problems and to share what counts and to practice our English, since my class is bilingual. When we do sharing, one student begins and is asked

"What's new?" This is not a question-and-answer time but usually a family time when students share things such as buying new shoes or a grandmother returning from Mexico or the death of a relative.

Our circle may take twenty minutes and varies each day. I like to do it in the morning when they seem most responsive to listening to each other. By the end of the year, they have become very adept at managing the circle without me. I enjoy the process the most when I am part of the audience. They are at the point where they can be respectful and remind each other of how to behave without calling me in to monitor. We also use this time for "fun" and for team-building activities.

The question about struggling to help students make good decisions once given choices is an incredible one. Their faces sometimes frown at the realization that the best or right thing to do doesn't always benefit them. Giving them the opportunity to work through this is ultimately the most valuable lesson. Seeing kids sacrifice for one another breaks my heart. When the opposite occurs, it is difficult to withhold my disappointment. With tenderness, I ask them how they felt about their decision. Many times those who don't feel good about it don't have much to say or are defensive.

A recent example took place because students were "losing" possessions. We talked about what to do if you "find" something like a quarter or a toy or a pencil. We discussed this for a while and eventually one student put together a box that sits on top of the aquarium. Anything that is found goes in the box and at the end of the day we try to find the owner. It was difficult for students at first but now it has become a routine and everyone is much happier. They can trust each other more.

Things do not always go the way I would like. For example, on a recent trip to the library, the class got very noisy. I was patiently waiting at the end of the line knowing that they would be able to work out the problem. By the time they did, it was too late to check out any books. They were crushed! They talked about it in a circle and have decided to change their behavior.

Another process that we have put in place is cleaning up the room. We asked the custodian to pass our room by so that we could take care of it. Learning to take care of the entire environment—physical, emotional, and academic—has been a great learning experience. Students no longer pass a piece of trash because it is not theirs. They pick it up and remind the class to be diligent.

My favorite example of students being intrinsically, actively engaged in meaningful, thoughtful learning occurred last year with my third and fourth graders. During one of our community meetings a safety issue came up. It turned out that students were being accosted in the local library in the afternoon. They felt powerless in solving this problem. "We're just kids, nobody will listen to us," Karla Gentle said. This was a fascinating discussion. Each student began to share their experiences. I asked them what could we do about this or if we should just not go to the library. We all agreed something should be done. This sparked a letter-writing campaign to the library, police department, and mayor's office. Students also designed posters and organized a march to the library. We carried our posters through the neighborhood, loudly alerting the community to our plight. Consequently we received individualized letters from the mayor, stating that patrols around the library after school would increase. A sheriff's department representative visited our classroom to discuss how to react toward strangers. We were then asked to speak before the city council and I did. The students could not go because it was so late at night. We were thanked for our concern and told that it had not been the first complaint but because it came from the kids, they paid more attention to it. They have increased their police patrols, and the students have noticed. I hope my students will never forget this true-to-life social studies lesson and their ability to make meaningful decisions.

Each year I learn more by giving up more control. Each year it feels safer to take another step into the realm of democracy in the classroom. Each success builds upon another!

2

The Curriculum Connection
Real Learning for Democratic Teaching

Our Invitation

The curriculum is often the cause of students' lack of interest. Hilton Smith, former director of Foxfire, who has many years of experience working with students who engage in project-centered learning, explains that when students engage in interdisciplinary work that is satisfying, their interest, enthusiasm, and level of learning increase dramatically. Authentic experiences that come from the students are essential for changing the paradigm.

Sharon Setoguchi expects her junior high students to be experts as they define *expertise*. Then, Carlos Lopez, a former student owner of Food From the 'Hood, shares his reflections. Kate Thomas then describes some practical skills to get projects started.

To Teachers and Their Students: The Question Is "How Can We Learn?," Not "What Are We Going to Do Today?"

Hilton Smith

Hilton taught high school social studies, worked in the Foxfire program, and currently masquerades as an Associate Professor of Education at Piedmont College in northeast Georgia.

Books and articles about classroom activities always seem to be written solely for teachers, who always seem to assume that they in turn are solely responsible for what goes on in the classroom. The reality is that students ultimately are responsible for their own learning, and they are as much in charge of what goes on in the classroom as their teachers. When we are honest with each other we acknowledge that reality. Because productive classroom work for worthwhile learning requires collaboration by everyone in the room, this chapter addresses students as well as teachers.

Teachers, if you are willing to involve your students by sharing this chapter with them and exploring its ideas, keep reading. Otherwise, bail out now.

Students, if you are willing to accept responsibility for your own learning and to work with your teacher in figuring out how to best get into the material of this course, keep reading. Otherwise, say so now. No need to waste everyone's time.

This chapter describes one kind of classroom work in an active learning approach that involves students and teacher in authentic work on the material to be learned in the course. Some topics are best dealt with in discussions; others seem ready-made for role playing and simulations; others for good old library and Internet research and a written report; and some, yes, for lecture and note taking. Many topics lend themselves to projects. Let's look at four examples of authentic project-based learning.

In a twelfth-grade government and economics class using *Time* magazine as the initial source of topics, one group of students learned about the compact between states in the southeast to rotate storage of nuclear wastes to each state in a preset order. Then they learned that one of the sites being considered next was in the mountainous county just across the state line from where they lived. They dug into the literature about nuclear wastes, then began attending the hearings being held in that county. They taped interviews with people attending the hearings, both residents and government agency representatives. By being informed about nuclear wastes, they could ask informed questions that could not be dismissed as "kid" questions. Their presence and questions actually affected the outcome of the hearings, which were canceled after only about half had been completed. During all this they reported back to the class (and other classes), so we all benefited from what they learned. We learned about politics and government and economics never found in a textbook or a teacher's lecture. It was durable, lifelong learning, not items for a multiple choice test.

A second-grade class in a rural area decided that it wanted to do a radio show in order to learn language arts skills, writing, editing, speaking, interviewing, and so on. The teacher had no background in radio, but she agreed to give it a try. The principal approved, sort of, but insisted that they had to keep up their assignments in the basal reader ("Dick and Jane"!). The students assaulted the basal reader, completing a whole week's work on Mondays, then worked on the radio show Tuesday through Friday during their language arts time. Each week they delivered a cassette of a complete thirty-minute radio show to the local radio station, which broadcast it on Saturday mornings. Virtually everyone in that community tuned in. The shows became more polished each week, as their language arts skills improved in ways that were demonstrable to the entire community. The members of that class wanted to learn in order to produce quality work for a real audience.

A teacher thought her sixth-grade class would be interested in storytelling as a language arts activity. Nope. They were concerned about the recent abduction and murder of a student their age nearby. Storytelling seemed, well, dumb. Working together, the teacher and students developed a language arts unit to produce literature on safety measures for people their age. The work was so much better than what the local authorities had developed that the county found funds to pay for reproduction and dissemination of the safety brochures. Their drive to create quality work led them to acquire language arts skills in ways that surprised even them.

In the Bay Area of California, the students in a combined third-fourth grade class pursued their (mostly) Asiatic heritages through a study of Angel Island, the immigration processing center through which many of their ancestors had passed. Not always a pleasant study, because Angel Island was rank with abuse, loneliness, and heartbreak. But it served as a guiding theme for virtually all their work for a year, work that helped them learn English, understand their own cultural heritages, and come to terms with the dominant culture in which they lived.

As these examples show, learning through projects does not involve assigning topics to groups of students (or even letting groups pick) to work on and then report to the class. In too many cases teachers assign what they call projects as a more entertaining, keep-busy solution to classroom management. Students' insights, skills, and knowledge are not involved. Projects come and go and are as forgettable as the usual teacher-directed, text-focused, test-driven stuff. More to the point, those projects rarely convey the excitement of inquiry, let alone the organizing concepts and methods of the academic disciplines they were presumably designed to teach.

So I am not talking about The Project Method, whereby the curriculum is to be learned by students doing project after project. That was tried some decades ago and earned a deservedly bad rap. Early in my teaching career I visited a classroom purportedly using The Project Method. The students had wrapped the entire inside of a classroom in sheets of white paper. The subject was Egypt. Each student had a section of a drawing of the inside of an Egyptian pyramid tomb to reproduce, so that when complete you would have the sense of being inside that tomb. Everyone was busy, "on task." But that's all that the study of Egypt was. The students did not know anything about Egypt or Egyptian history. Some of them did not even know whose tomb it was. Nor did they know why they were reproducing the inside of a pharaoh's tomb. This was not an example of authentic project-based learning. Rather, it was a typical example of The Project Method. It is an example of what to avoid.

Then what should it look like? The major principles of active, authentic learning are listed below. Read each principle. What difference would establishing these make in how this class does its work? We need to hear from everyone so that we can agree on what these mean for us as a class.

1. The "work" of classroom instruction, students' and teachers' work, generates knowledge as information, meaning, and insights. The point is not to "cover" a bunch of stuff over a designated period of time. Both students and teachers have to get out of that mind-set before you can attempt any kind of active learning, especially projects.

2. This approach builds on participatory decision making. Everyone has a voice in deciding how the work is to be done and done well.

3. Maintain a firm focus on academic goals (state, district, and your own personal). Use the working techniques, or methods, of the academic disciplines such as math, history, science, or literary criticism. If it's a history project, work like historians, not like drudges sifting through textbooks. Not sure what historians do? Then acquiring those techniques, even in the forms appropriate for lower-grade levels, becomes part of the overall strategy.

4. Maintain a combination of high expectations for quality work and full support to achieve those expectations. What we are talking about here is *performance,* not just getting stuff done. Work on projects as approximations of professional work, as scholarly work.

5. Projects encourage the development of habits of mind, like patience, openness to new ideas, appreciation of others' work. Be conscious of changes in yourselves as those values become part of how you deal with the world.

6. Understand that grades are not an effective motivator for long-term, durable learning or intellectual commitment to academic work. In fact, grubbing for grades tends to have just the opposite effect: learn for the test, then forget it, go on to the next unit. Authentic work should not be soiled by emphasis on grades. But it does need to be assessed for strong points (achievement) and what needs improvement (growth). Therefore, reflections, assessments, and evaluations are part of the authentic project, not just tests at the end of the units. More on this later.

7. Relevance is in the eye of the beholder. That means that students decide what is relevant to them. I read in education texts, and hear teachers talk, about "making the material relevant to the students." None of us can make anything relevant to others. We search for relevance together. Teachers guide that search. Students join the search by being willing to stretch themselves to give authentic work a try.

8. Work like this requires us to use our imaginations, something that most schooling tends to stifle. First there is imagining how a topic could be learned in some way other than the way you usually do it. Then there is imagining what this work might look like when you are done. Then there is instrumental imagination: What exactly do we do? What do we need? What problems might we encounter? How are we going to do this? How will we know whether it is any good?

"But," you say, "we do have to cover a bunch of stuff over a designated period of time, and there are grades, and we have those god-awful standardized tests!" Acknowledged. From my own practice and from the practice of Foxfire-influenced practitioners I can assert this: If teachers and their students agree to open themselves to possibilities of this approach and pursue it with determination and care, all those givens you just threw at me can be achieved and you can go way beyond them in depth. What we notice is that we become more efficient with practice, so meeting those requirements is no problem. Not only that, schooling done this way begins to seem really worthwhile.

Features of Authentic Project-based Learning

An authentic project is like jazz. There's a basic structure: rhythm, chords, maybe a theme that keeps us together. The performance combines improvisation with that structure. Support roles pass around to keep the structure; everyone gets solo time. When the piece starts no one knows exactly where it will go or what the final performance will look like until we're done. Yes, sometimes it just breaks down. Someone plays the wrong chord, or somehow we lose the rhythm. Stop. Debrief: What happened? Try again. In jazz, everyone is a learner, all the time. Jazz players see performance as practice, practice as performance.

Jazz injects an element of unpredictability into the work that students usually handle better than teachers. Students, document your work and push each other for quality work, which will reassure anxious teachers.

An authentic project is a work in progress, which means that until it is completed, you never know for sure just exactly how it will turn out. That's difficult for some of our more compulsive folks (students and teachers alike) to handle. That's fine, because in cooperative work, the visions of the creative, spontaneous folks can be focused by the duty-driven folks.

Mistakes are to learn from. But make sure the mistakes are identified and discussed. Figure out what is needed to avoid it next time.

Active learning is not politically neutral. It asserts that everyone's voice is relevant and that therefore it is everyone's responsibility to know what they are talking about. That also means that sometimes projects venture into politically sensitive areas. In Illinois, a group of fifth graders doing an ecology project on the lake in their town park traced pollutants in the water to a major industry in the area, an industry with political clout in that town. The political stuff hit the fan. It was a tough time for everyone for several months. But the students' work withstood scrutiny, and they provided the industry an opportunity to respond, so eventually the issue was settled and the polluting stopped. Just be aware of the ripple effect of doing authentic work. Plan ahead. Think of ways to limit adverse reactions that might kill your chances of finishing the project or of doing other projects later. Rule #1: Do not surprise your principal.

Thinking in strategies. We all tend to become accustomed to daily and weekly lesson plans designed by the teacher such as "What are we going to do on Wednesday?" The teacher has to get out of that lesson-plan mind-set and into a different approach: Here's where these students are now, I know where we should be by the end of the semester, so what can we do to get us from here to there?

Work away from hypothetical, content-coverage assignments; work toward the kind of performance activities of the school band, drama groups, and athletic teams. Reminder: Few groups of students arrive in the room with a full set of skills and attitudes for effective group work. Few teachers come in with the skills to help create and encourage it. It takes time to develop a collaborative, cooperative climate in a classroom. Since projects usually require this, a central strategy question for the whole group is "What kinds of things could we be doing now that will build such a collaborative, cooperative climate in our room?"

The student responsibility is to get out of the "What are we going to do today?" mind-set and open yourselves to the opportunities of extended work that you help design. Be honest in debriefings about what could be done better and about what you need to work on to improve the quality of the work. There are schools where it is uncool to be interested in schoolwork. If you are in one of those schools, you have to be willing to buck the conventions. The more you support each other, the easier that will be.

The role of the teacher is to stimulate, supervise, inform, assist, and insist on quality. The more of those roles students accept as their responsibility, the more satisfying it will be. And those are exactly the kind of skills and attitudes that breed success in the workplace.

Don't expect projects to be trouble-free. Do expect occasional loss of focus and momentum, sometimes after several days of productive activity and enthusiasm. Expect occasional tensions between teacher and students, between students, maybe between the class and other classes. Too much energy at school is spent smothering tensions, many of which are caused by the school itself. Where else are we supposed to learn how to work with tensions, to realize that tensions are as natural as day and night? Authentic projects generate tensions, so part of everyone's job is to attend to them.

Having fun is not the point, but may be a by-product. The point is, is the project worthwhile? Did we learn stuff that will stick with us so we can handle the next level of material whenever and wherever that is? Did we do quality work? If the answer is "yes" to those, and if the work was enjoyable, absorbing, and interesting, then call it fun.

To Make Sure a Project Succeeds

Projects are best when they are spontaneous, spun out of the work already going on or from genuine interest. But, thinking in strategies here, teachers and students need to learn how to build projects based on interest. Consider starting with "project-ettes," small, quick inquiries into small, discrete topics. For example, while studying the Bill of Rights, which generates all sorts of opinions about the right to bear arms, freedom of speech, and arrest rights, everyone takes an issue, frames a couple of interview questions, then questions ten students and ten adults, and reports the results back to the class. Then build up to more ambitious projects as you move on to the next topics.

The pivot point comes when we imagine the project: what we think will be the end product or performance or result; what each of us will do to get us there; what resources we will need. Conventional schooling seems to turn off imagination, so you might have to practice to regain it. While planning the project, get everyone involved. Do not let a few students dominate. Provide opportunities for everyone to participate and even to lead.

Do not rely on projects as the primary way for students to teach the class important material until (a) the quality and depth are sound and reliable, (b) everyone in the class agrees that they are ready to try it, and (c) they hold each other to a high standard. That takes some doing.

Models, modeling. What is there that could be used as a guide or standard to shoot for? The best models are those that come from the academic disciplines being studied. That also means that the criteria for adequate and superior performance come not from the teacher's subjective judgments, but from the work of those in the field. Not sure how to go about that? Enlist the pros. You probably will be surprised how agreeable they are to help.

An example: For a ninth-grade geography class, I presented a circumnavigation of the globe on the south fortieth parallel, combining a taped narrative-with-music soundtrack with slides and opaque projector visuals from books; there were four stops for questions and to ask "What did you notice about _____?" and "Why do you think they farm that way?" For the debriefing I focused on (a) geographic concepts (land-human relations, regions, climate zones, and so on) and (b) qualities of the performance, What worked and why? That performance became the benchmark for students to aim for in their own studies of selected parallels.

Build a repertoire of skills and criteria for quality work. What do we need to know in order to do this and do it well? Some classes develop a playbook of ideas, criteria, resources, dos and don'ts. Think quality; think beauty.

To assess is to find out what has been learned or how things are going. Assess the process of the project; assess each piece or phase of work; assess knowledge, skills, attitudes, progress. We all need feedback on how well we are doing and on exactly what we need to do to improve. That's assessment. Evaluation is to assign a value, a grade, in other words, to an assessment. Students should participate in developing the criteria for assessing and evaluating projects. It is an important skill to master. Expect your initial efforts to be crude and gapped, then to improve with subsequent projects. Learn how to be critical friends for each other, so you can help each other improve the work. That involves trust, so maybe you have to take some time to develop it.

Work together to decide which assessments are to be used for grades. Try to stick with those which can be documented. "CYA" is still the law of the school jungle at most schools. Peg grades to a C. That is, adequate, passing performance on all parts of the project gets you a C. In other words, just completing the project does not get an automatic A. Bs and As then require either superior performance on all parts, or something beyond what was involved in the C work.

A very big challenge: Do not limit the assessments to what was supposed to be learned, that is, what was taught. That's important, for sure, but it is just as important to find out what everyone learned that was not in the curriculum. And when you figure out how to do this really well, be sure to share it with the rest of educationdom, because, frankly, we do not do this well at all.

Debrief. Individuals, teams, the whole class. Early, midway, in lulls and downtimes, and at the end. Informal: "Did you guys sort out who will interview Ms. Lee?" Quasi-formal: "Everyone focus up here for a moment. Have any of the teams found sources that might help other teams?" More formal: "Take ten minutes to jot down what you think are the most important six things you've learned from this project. We'll use those to construct a master list, including what to do different next time." In a very real way, learning is locked into place by debriefing, especially the final debriefing, where you try to figure what worked well and what needs improvement. What did we learn about the topic? What did we learn about ourselves?

While teachers most often assume responsibility for debriefings, there is no reason why students should not assume increasing responsibility for initiating debriefings. There is a good reason for students to learn how to do that: when you debrief you have to think, so you learn another dimension of thinking. And student-led debriefings, without the teacher necessarily present, often lead to more honest assessments of the work. That usually leads to more quality work.

Learning requires reflection. We have become so busy, so entertained, so self-absorbed, that maybe we have forgotten how to reflect. To answer those debriefing questions above you have to look honestly into yourself, then share what you see with your community of learners. That is not always comfortable but it really is essential for learning. The teacher's role in reflection is to stimulate, guide, and model reflection. The students' role is to open yourselves to it. Forget attitudes and postures. Just think about the work and be guided by the teacher's prompts. It takes time, but after a while you will reflect on all sorts of things in your lives.

How to Know If a Project Is Working

- It seems to have a life of its own—that is, you continue it, talk it, argue it, defend it, refine it, expand it, contract it, and so forth. You feel like you "own" the topic.
- You keep seeing ways to improve it. New possibilities keep popping into your head as the work progresses.
- Each person feels empowered to stop the work to request that the group deal with a problem.
- The work provides for the loners (I am one of those) as well as the gatherers and socializers. The students who usually dominate classroom work pull back and provide spaces for less assertive members. Everyone's opinions are considered, and everyone tries to present opinions worth considering. No one is dissed.

You are aware that you are learning and that what you are learning is durable and useful. The material is not "covered," it is learned. It becomes a piece of your worldview. You realize that you understand how a part of the world operates that you never knew before, maybe did not even know existed.

Students as Experts

Sharon Setoguchi

Sharon teaches English, Japanese, and Journalism at Stephen M. White Middle School in the Los Angeles Unified School District.

One of the greatest challenges facing classroom teachers today is motivation—how to get students involved in the learning experiences of the classroom. I teach middle school language arts, and I began using projects as a way to get students involved in what we were studying. I discovered that students would perform much the same on the projects I assigned as they did on any other assignment. They would do just what I asked—no more, no less. I had to ask myself why students did not seem to care about what we were working on. Reflecting on my own learning as an adult gave me a better understanding of how to help my students become more motivated.

One of my passions is rubber stamping. Creating beautiful cards or wall hangings is something I take great pride in. Learning how to make more and more intricate pieces is something I can happily spend hours doing. While I don't consider myself an "expert," I certainly feel that I have some expertise in this craft.

Thinking about this gave me the idea of what I call The Expert Project. At the beginning of the school year, I asked students to brainstorm what makes someone an expert in any particular field. Through class discussion, the students began to understand that it takes time, dedication, and much study to become an expert. We then brainstormed the ways in which a person can acquire expertise. Here is the list the students developed:

- Reading
- Research
- Practice
- Using the scientific method of hypothesis and testing
- Interviewing experts
- Watching experts
- Examining the work of experts

I then asked my students to list three or four topics that they would be genuinely interested in becoming experts on. Their task would be to gain expertise in an area of their choice. I did not require that they focus on academic studies; anything they wanted to become "experts" at was fine. Once they had some topics in mind, I asked them to find

33

others who had similar areas of interest. After some negotiation of topics, students formed self-selected groups of three or four.

Next, we needed to make a decision about how much time to spend
on this project. The class decided that one month would allow the students time to research their topic and locate experts in the field whom
they could interview. We also agreed to evaluate their progress after
two weeks to see if one month was enough time for them to do a quality job. I explained that I was available as a resource and trou-
bleshooter. If they encountered problems as they tried to gain expertise,
we would try to find solutions to their problems by working together.

Together, students and I set four requirements for this project.

1. Demonstrate their expertise to the class with some sort of presen-
    tation.
2. Use at least three different resources: books, periodicals, and
    experts in their field.
3. Create an annotated bibliography for their topic.
4. Write a one-page "extract" of their project.

Most students chose to do most of their preliminary research at the
public library. Books and periodicals formed the basis for their initial
investigations. One problem students had was narrowing their topic.
They soon realized that four weeks was not enough time to become
experts on very much. After only a few days of research, many of them
realized that they would have to revise their own expectations of the
process. One student even became discouraged, saying that she could
never become an expert on anything in that short amount of time. We
discussed as a class the difference between being an expert who has
acquired mastery and being someone who has some degree of expertise or is on their way to having such expertise.

Once their initial research had begun, I asked each group to come
up with three or four questions, which we called Essential Questions,
that would guide the rest of their study. What was it that was really
important for them to know? What had they discovered from their preliminary research that they wanted to know about in more depth? Was
there anything that they were now intrigued about that they could not
find answered in the books or periodicals they had read? Narrowing
their topic to only three or four Essential Questions made them focus
on a very specific area of study and would prepare them for their
expert interview.

In order to find experts on their chosen topics, students used a variety of sources. Some students used someone in their family or circle of
friends that they knew. Others called local universities or professional
guilds. Another group called the local chamber of commerce. One

group of students studying international cooking even called local restaurants and asked to speak to the head chef!

As students began their search for experts to interview, one problem they encountered was difficulty in contacting an expert and arranging for an interview. After much discussion, we realized that telephone etiquette was a skill that many of them had not been taught. They realized they needed to learn how to sound professional. We discussed prefacing their phone call with a well-written business letter saying that they would be calling. They practiced their part of the telephone conversation in class. Many students also practiced at home with parents or older siblings. One student even asked her parent to take the role of an uncooperative secretary.

Our next discussion centered around the importance of planning their interviews. Students used their Essential Questions to develop their interview questions. I emphasized the need to have their questions ready before making their initial contact with the expert. With their questions in hand, many students were able to conduct telephone interviews once they had practiced their telephone skills. Other students used tape recorders and arranged to meet their expert to conduct the interview.

As I watched students become involved in this project, I realized the value of allowing students to choose any topic, no matter how unrelated to traditional school subjects, for their project. Because these were areas of study that truly interested my students, there was no problem with motivation. One group of young women chose cosmetics as their field. They originally began their expert study on ways to apply makeup. As they began their research, they found a lot of information about harmful ingredients in the cosmetics many of them used. When they presented their final project, they included information on the safe use of cosmetics and how to make sure that the cosmetics you use do not contain ingredients that are not good for your skin.

After they had conducted interviews, students were reminded to go back to the books and periodicals they had found. With all of their information in one place, they were now ready to collate their data and plan their presentations. Once again, their Essential Questions formed a type of outline from which they could work. Some groups even revised their questions in order to include new information they had discovered. I introduced various ways to organize the information, including graphic organizers and index cards. Students chose the way they found the easiest or most convenient.

Presentations ranged from demonstrations and student-produced videos to minilectures complete with handouts. While we did not discuss presentation formats as a class, students were told that whatever form of presentation they wanted to use was acceptable. The goal, I reminded students, was to demonstrate to the class that they had acquired some level of expertise. For the most part, students used presentation styles that they had seen or used for other classes. Selecting an appropriate format was quite natural for the students—some topics readily lent themselves to demonstrations, while others required a more formal presentation.

After all the presentations were over, students were asked to reflect on their learning as individuals rather than as a group. I asked students to evaluate their learning based on five questions that had been my own Essential Questions as we embarked on this project:

1. What have you discovered about the term "expert"?
2. What is required to be an "expert"?
3. What level of expertise did you reach personally?
4. What skills did you develop that you can use in future projects or classes?
5. Did you enjoy the project? If so, what made your learning enjoyable?

It is the sense of expertise that I feel with my rubber stamping hobby that I wanted my students to experience. My hope was that students would use reading, writing, speaking, and listening skills to acquire expertise and improve their language skills through the process of becoming an expert. I think that this project successfully met these goals. Students became engaged learners as they worked on becoming experts. They learned to research a topic, contact and interview primary sources, synthesize and present information, and speak in front of an audience.

For me, this is the kind of "active learning" that Hilton Smith refers to in his chapter. With each step I take and each project I embark on with my students, I want to continue the conversation about what is important to them and where they need and want to acquire expertise in their own lives. In this way, I believe we will find even more opportunities for the kind of active learning that is truly motivating for students.

What Food From the 'Hood Has Done

Carlos Lopez

Carlos graduated from Crenshaw High School and has returned to help Food From the 'Hood begin franchising.

In 1992, Los Angeles erupted in a riot. The police officers who had been filmed physically abusing Rodney King were found innocent of police brutality by a jury in Simi Valley. Damage to some neighborhoods was extensive as Los Angeles experienced curfews and a state of fear. Students at Crenshaw High School, a Los Angeles Unified school, decided they had to respond. Carlos Lopez describes the hands-on social action that developed as a response to this horrific set of events.

Food From the 'Hood is a student-owned business located at Crenshaw High School in Los Angeles. In 1992, we created a campus garden and began selling produce at farmers' markets. In 1994, we introduced our first salad dressing.

Our company mission is as follows:

- Create jobs for youth
- Prove that businesses can be environmentally friendly, socially responsible, and profitable
- Show what young adults can accomplish, and
- Use this experience to prepare for the future.

Company "profits" provide college scholarships for the student-owners. We still sell our produce at farmers' markets and 25 percent of our crops is donated to feed the needy in our community.

I got involved in Food From the 'Hood in 1993 when I was a sophomore. Food From the 'Hood began in 1992 when a biology teacher decided to get her students involved in a garden. She had five classes and enlisted ten students from each class. We began as a program to give something back to the community. We raised fresh produce and sold some of it for scholarship money and gave the rest to shelters. The damage during the riots was mostly to businesses so this process was to help get students money not as employment but as a way to earn scholarship money.

Our biology teacher knew that a hands-on approach was what would get students committed. We began with student-owners of the company and worked mostly after school. The garden brought different kinds of kids together, and it was a new place to meet people. We developed friendships and bonds and have made friends for life. We learned from each other and from working together and from the team activities we did. But we also saw the rewards for what we did. We cherished it more and we stayed interested. We all worked hard to do our best.

When we began, it was only a garden and we only made six hundred dollars the first year. That was not enough money to help anyone with college so we got connected to the business world and did research. We decided to start a company and manufacture Italian salad dressing. We're still a small company with student owners and interns but we like working for our education.

I suppose that one of the things I like best is the mixture of so many kinds of kids. Some have 4.0 grade-point averages and others have 1.5s. Some play sports. The best football player in the school is a co-owner. But the garden and the company have broadened all of our minds, past our own neighborhood and into other cities and other races. We have a new vision for ourselves. All the kids have been accepted into four-year colleges. Some kids did not want to apply because they did not think they could get in. But the company helps students with tutoring and support and helps raise everyone's self-esteem. And now we have one franchise and two more planned. We made $100,000 last year. Any of us could work anywhere now.

Food From the 'Hood is so important to us. It's good peer pressure. We don't want to be left out. Our advisors have been supportive, but they know we can do the job. They have encouraged us to do what we needed to do but they let us do it. They never did it for us and in that sense they have been friends. Food From the 'Hood is much more than a company that produces healthy and delicious dressings. It's a process that has given life to many of the students.

The Elusive Project

Kate Thomas

Kate is currently a graduate student and substitute teacher in Los Angeles.

Teachers, you have been challenged to involve your students in the process of their own education. Students, you have been invited to use your voice in determining your own education. Projects offer the kind of relevant learning we want for and from each other, but Hilton Smith is right when he describes the elusive essence of a relevant project. This piece focuses on some practical advice for getting started.

Project. The term is a loaded one. It conjures up all sorts of images: from following oodles of instructions to a chance to goof off while one person does most of the work. I know because I was schooled and I've done the schooling. I've been bored and frustrated from both sides of the table with what the well-intentioned "project" was meant to do—involve the students and teacher, passionately. A real project requires significant risk taking, trust, and ongoing planning, elements that are often missing.

Risk Taking and Trust

Risk taking is an interesting phenomenon. Most of us took huge risks when we learned, for example, to walk, talk, use the toilet, and eat with a knife, fork, and spoon. We learned even as we made mistakes. We kept at it even if we were being laughed at, ignored, or even scolded, because we were motivated. Projects cannot be successful if everyone isn't motivated.

In order to take risks, we have to trust ourselves and the people we're working with, and be given choices about what we want. Creating an environment where everyone feels safe takes time and practice. Chapter 5 talks more about this. But a way to begin is with quick gamelike activities that are deliberately designed to increase individual risk taking in a trusting environment. (Remember that each of us defines risk in very personal ways.) For example, the class leads a blindfolded volunteer (soldier) across an area littered with objects (minefield) using words only. The group works together to accomplish their task, discovering, for example, that everyone talking at the same time is not helpful. To debrief the activity, an essential question or two is asked. For example, "What are three things that helped the soldier's trek?" or " . . . three things that made it more difficult?" A running list of responses is kept and posted in the room. This activity may be integrated into a unit on the Civil War to enliven the curricular content. The

39

practice and experience of cooperation serve as powerful metaphors that can be referenced again and again. Cooperative games are a kinesthetic learning experience and an invaluable addition to lectures and book learning. And, when everyone starts talking at the same time a week later, all anyone has to say is, "Whoa! I see a minefield!"

How does this kind of activity build trust and promote risk taking? As the class works to solve problems that are fun and "pretend," they are experiencing decision making, sharing, problem solving, and compromise. They are working to create norms, secure commitments, generate participation, and create a purposeful mission, skills necessary for creating democratic projects in the classroom.

Planning

As the environment becomes trusting and safe, planning, planning, and planning must happen. The most valuable planning tools are masking tape, easel paper, and colored markers. The kids and I use these tools almost every day when we teach to create a written history of where we've been and where we're going. The advantage is that we can save it, look at it down the road, laugh at it, spur reflection and assessment and evaluation with it, build things with it, take bits of it home, and, yes, even throw it away! Chart everything.

I envision projects as planning triathlons. The first event is the *brief.* A brief is to a project what a business plan is to a small business; the brief is the process that gives an idea voice. The second event in the triathlon is the *activity,* that is, the implementation stage of turning a project from plan to product. The *debrief* is the final event in the triathlon, or the reflection and evaluation stage. A debrief is the closure that illuminates, highlights, and emphasizes such things as weaknesses, strengths, quality, quantity, growth, traits, patterns, and the "next time . . ." questions. I will focus on the brief because it will determine, to a large extent, the activity and debrief.

It can be difficult to know when an opportunity for a project presents itself; experience develops this skill. A project can be mark-set-go by an array of instigations, from a seemingly silly question to an administrative edict, from a habit to a hobby, from a current event to a schoolmate's suicide. Keep it simple—start small—take seriously Smith's advice about first trying a "project-ette." Build your skills and make the first experiences with the process successful.

So, something's come up. An opportunity has presented itself. The time is ripe. Begin by lining out a simple column chart with the headings Problem and Solution. (Other examples are Given and Then or Question and Answer. Be creative.) A third column, Concerns, is very useful as the "yes, but" thinkers keep us in check. During brainstorming, phrase the ideas ("paper pickup," "paint day," "plant flowers") to prevent getting caught up by adjectives and descriptions and losing the imaginative flow. Remember, because you do a chart doesn't mean you have to do a project. Filling in a chart is an important lesson in itself. Play around with this. Go slow. Be comfortable. Push the envelope gently and pull a little harder than that.

Next, take the center column ideas—the "solutions"—and list each on a second chart, leaving a lot of space between each item. Invite students to add the whos, whats, whens, and wheres of each, jotting down a few descriptors when appropriate. Then add the hows and whys. The point is to clarify serious ideas in order to begin negotiating.

Gaining Consensus

When ready for the process of selecting a project, simple majority-wins voting is the easiest, and usually the tool most teachers use. This is OK, especially for minor decisions within projects. Gaining a true democratic vote—*consensus*—can be extremely time consuming, frustrating, and takes heaps of practice. I warn you now, though, that by gaining consensus you probably avoid the major hurdle to creating a successful project, and for a very important reason. Since everyone will be affected by the project, everyone needs to commit. If some of the people have no commitment, then you can expect either little quality work from them, the most subtle of underminings, or the grandest of coups d'état.

If you'd like to try achieving consensus, remember: it's a negotiation. In simple majority-rules, most of the people are ecstatic while some of the people are mad; this is *not* consensus. The goal of consensus is everyone agreeing, everyone getting some of what they want, and giving up a little as well (even if it means some components of an idea are modified). Negotiation deepens a project's potential quality of success in so many ways.

So, in the name of consensus, create a skinny column next to the "solutions" listed and try a method called Thumbs. As each item is announced, every member in the class simply votes with a thumb up for "yes! let's go for it!" or down for "no! I can't live with this idea" or sideways for "I don't feel strongly either way." If you have to deal with saboteurs, take a strong look at the degree of emotional safety with individual members in your group. Maybe some work with cooperative games is in order? Thumbs down means the idea is out (we're trying to get everyone to buy in here). Of course negotiations, debates, pros, cons, and defenses will most likely ensue. People are allowed to change their mind, and revotes may be cast. It can be a long process. People get angry or silly and usually a bit of both. Think of this kind of voting process as the difference between caucus and election and remember that, after this, synergy is on your side.

Once the class has decided on a project, the next step is the activity. The project can change in many ways as the class proceeds and sometimes needs your coaxing when tasks do not work out easily or smoothly. The debrief process should happen frequently, using reflection to get at what is working, what is not, and how everyone feels. Trusting the students is important.

So, projects are for everyone. Projects are only one way. Projects are a powerful way to envision, practice, and experience democracy. Drawing these parallels between democracy and project are, hopefully, obvious and apparent. It's not what we do, but how we do it (gosh, I sound like my mother!) that make the memories count. Carry on!

3

Consensus and
Decision Making

Our Invitation

This chapter addresses consensus and democratic classrooms. What are the levels of democracy and where can you start? How do you ask students to make decisions without voting? Jeff Haas and his students from the Downtown Business Magnets High School share their experiences in sharing power and making decisions together. Terry O'Connor's thoughtful ideas and experience will help you move toward consensus and create a sense of shared responsibility in the class.

The Rhythms and Routines
of Democratic Classrooms

Terry O'Connor

Terry is the director of the Center for Teaching and Learning at Indiana State University, Terre Haute.

Ask people what democratic education means and you will receive all sorts of answers. Some will give a cautious look and warn that it is a naive invitation to chaos. These are what Barbara Coloroso (1994) called "brick wall" teachers. They take a firm stand on what subjects should be covered and how students must act. Any diversions from their tasks are seen as ramblings that will, sooner or later, run smack into the hard reality epitomized by their educational wall.

For others, democratic pedagogy is an invitation to a nurturing freedom. Unshackled from the bureaucratic grind, these educators encourage the blossoming of native learning curiosity. Coloroso warns, however, that many of these teachers fall into a "jellyfish" pedagogy, one that responds to a child's wants more than their needs.

While the arguments between brick wall and jellyfish versions of education may be the most common ones, they serve to obscure the heritage of educators who have tried to democratize teaching and learning in our schools. They have developed three distinct ways of approaching democratic schooling (O'Connor 1997).

The more conservative approach to democratic education has focused on teaching students political lessons that explain the values and structures of American democracy. Schools are seen as serving an invaluable function by preparing students as citizens. Reforms inspired by this approach have emphasized subjects like social studies and government and have encouraged student governments.

For some, however, political education is not enough. Modern democracies require social education in the arts of democratic living. Classrooms should become sites where students practice and learn these skills. This second approach has promoted cooperative learning, multicultural education, service learning, as well as supported a number of learner-centered pedagogies.

The third approach to democratic education calls on educators to recognize the underlying social structures on which schools and community are organized. Schooling can be a subversive or a liberating experience. Teachers and students must learn to be responsible for choosing democratic relationships when they work together. These educators have encouraged conflict resolution and peace education, diversity education programs, as well as critical pedagogy.

Confronted by three very different choices, a parent or teacher who wishes to be more democratic is right to feel somewhat confused. Where is the common ground? How can these grand ideals become real classroom practice? What are the guiding principles that have emerged from a century of democratic experiments?

It is best to begin with the lessons in how democractic methods offer better ways to address the social relationships of the classroom. Richard and Patricia Schmuck (1997) have pulled together the research on social identity, group formation, friendships, power relations, and other dimensions of social life, and documented how democratic techniques such as team building, collaborative learning, decision making, and conflict resolution make classrooms more effective. For many teachers, these are becoming familiar ideas, if not trusted practices. Techniques that address the social dimension of the classroom provide comfortable starting places for traditional teachers to begin democratizing their classroom practice.

A more difficult hurdle arises when teachers have to consider how to approach academic tasks democratically. How should the curriculum be redesigned? How do lessons change? What happens to the role of teacher? The lessons from progressive education are more hidden in this area. Popular methods, such as cooperative learning, appear to be fads rather than an advance in our understanding of the educational process. Yet, past democratic educators have shown how their teaching methods employ fundamental knowledge of teaching and learning to make their students more successful.

Finding a Democratic Rhythm

The school year has a rhythm that teachers and students recognize. Some classes have a weekly rhythm. There are even daily rhythms. These rhythms may lay just below our consciousness; they are powerful organizers of our educational relations.

John Dewey (1990) summarized one of the most important breakthroughs of democratic educators in the first part of the century with an essay called "The Child and the Curriculum." He describes the important difference between two educational camps: the content-oriented teachers and the student-oriented ones. Each relies on a different rhythm to plan, teach, and evaluate their students.

Democratic educators aim to connect their methods to the deep rhythms of natural learning rather than, say, the mechanical rhythms of a bell system. Since the turn of the century, they have used the knowledge of student growth and development to design educational settings.

Unfortunately, in the struggle over the direction of schooling, it was the content-oriented educators who were able to define the rhythm of our schools. The content-oriented rhythm of the school is found in the way educators plan around the text, measuring progress by the number of chapters covered. It is driven by lesson plans organized to cover subject matter. It is evaluated by how much content students can repeat. As a result, the learner-oriented teacher is surrounded by an organizational culture whose underlying patterns run contrary to their democratic initiatives.

So powerful are the content-oriented rhythms of the school that many educators find it difficult to imagine how to put their democratic values into practice. They recognize, intuitively, that learner-centered pedagogy breaks many of the habits of school. Time spent in team building activities may be considered wasted because students are not working on content. Student mistakes may be viewed as failure to master content. Lessons organized as projects may be criticized as taking time away from the official curriculum (the one supposedly tested on standardized exams). Organizing educational experiences around learning rhythms puts teachers at odds with the taken-for-granted expectations of those around them.

The rhythms of democratic learning experiences, if we were allowed to explore them in schools, provide a different way to organize educational activities. Instead of content, student growth and development become the markers for activities. Lesson plans are designed around changes in learners rather than content coverage. Evaluations are constructed to reveal personal strengths and areas for improvement. Without an understanding of how to construct activities around these alternative rhythms, however, the commitment to students and democracy appears more idealistic than practical, an accusation frequently aimed at progressive teachers. Ironically, it is precisely because democratic rhythms capitalize on natural learning process that they actually provide a more practical way to teach. The challenge is to find which of these models provides rhythms that best suit a particular teacher, students, and content.

A Democratic Teaching Rhythm

Democratic educators have devised a number of learner-centered models that are sophisticated enough to meet most teachers' needs to plan, conduct, and evaluate lessons. Rhythms can be developed from theories of personal, interpersonal, and intellectual development. John Dewey's theory of experience describes how people change their understanding of the world; it provides a rhythm for planning alternative approaches to the classroom. Jean Piaget's developmental stages support constructivist pedagogy. The Montessori method is based on a model of child development. The social psychology that has evolved from Kurt Lewin's research has led to cooperative learning approaches.

Paulo Freire developed ideas about social alienation into the phases of liberatory pedagogy. William Glasser's quality schools begin with a psychology of needs, while Daniel Goleman's recent work on emotional intelligence provides a guide for designing lessons that promote the affective growth of students. Grounding classroom experiences in models of human growth provides teachers with some clear guidelines for organizing lessons and managing classroom interactions.

Learner-centered teachers also define their subject matter along a continuum of progress. By laying out points of accomplishment and understanding the transitions between them, teachers can diagnose the capabilities of their students and plan a teaching rhythm that will lead students from that point to the next higher one. In this way, democratic educators convert theories of growth and models of the subject matter into a vision of the learning path students must travel, one that determines the appropriate rhythms for teaching and learning activities.

For example, once a teacher has decided which stage of development to address with the students, he or she can begin to use a rhythm such as the following generic one to plan a learning unit. The first phase in teaching a group of students should be a discovery one. Activities need to be designed that allow the teacher to get to know students' beliefs, skills, prior understandings, learning styles, social abilities, or other qualities (just what you need to know is usually contained in the personal development model being used). When the teacher has helped students understand their current ideas and beliefs, the teacher can make decisions about which direction to go.

At this point, the teacher moves into the second phase, the learning phase. Now the teacher must design activities that change the way that students understand and act on the world. Most democratic approaches rely on a series of learning cycles that engage students in actively processing new ideas in terms of their prior experiences. These cycles are carried out until students reach a particular level of expertise. The learning phase is characterized by the more precise routines for guiding learning cycles.

The third phase in this general rhythm begins when students are capable of applying their new abilities to situations where they can demonstrate their competence. When students can begin to produce performances, projects, exhibitions, or undertake studies or services, they engage in a stage of learning where knowledge is deeply internalized. They also understand how the learning can enhance their lives and create stronger communities. Teachers must provide activities that promote these connections.

This generic rhythm can be made more specific by adopting a particular pedagogical approach. Using learner-centered rhythms such as this, teachers can plan how to move students through the phases of an educational program and can evaluate students' progress in each phase and modify instructional activities to suit the best pace for them. The learner-centered teacher is tuning in to their personal, social, and intellectual development, in stark contrast to the relentless pace of grading periods organized to cover content.

It has been the loss of these guiding patterns that has been one of the real costs of discarding the heritage of democratic education that developed in the first half of this century. The educator who wishes to move beyond the idealistic commitment to democratic pedagogy must discover a learner-centered model around which to construct the rhythms guiding the classroom.

A Democratic Teaching Routine

The larger rhythms of learning programs have within them the smaller, more precise patterns that guide immediate interactions. For the sake of clarity, these rhythms can be called *routines*. Like formal lesson plans, teaching routines can map out the exact steps for coordinating actions. There are vital differences between the routines used by content-oriented teachers and those used by learner-centered teachers.

Of course the dominant paradigm recommends routines that link motivation to the content through rewards or punishments based on content mastery. Teachers plan their work with students in terms of the amount of content addressed. Even when allowing small group work, traditional teachers are uncertain of its instructional value. They cannot imagine how student talk and student work is part of the learning process. By contrast, democratic routines for using groups help students reach certain stages along the developmental continuum. They are part of the overall rhythm.

Knowledge of learner-centered classroom routines can be one of the most important tools for a democratic teacher because they give specific shape to their teaching ideals. They explain how to organize the work teachers and students do together. Routines provide the detailed planning guide for the larger rhythms of the lesson. There are, for example, routines for the discovery phase, others for the learning phase, and still others for the application phase. A sample routine described below is suited for the learning phase. It illustrates the kind of structure that democratic teachers can use to guide their classrooms without sacrificing responsiveness to student development.

David Kolb's learning styles model (1984) assumes that learners must process information in four stages before assimilating it well. A teacher's role is to organize lessons so that students have the opportunity to engage in each of these stages.

His approach begins with learners' concrete experiences. The teacher draws examples, presents a situation, and gives models or pictures that connect to students' lives. The aim of the teacher is to elicit descriptive statements, the kind that invite every learner in the class into the conversation. For example, a teacher might ask students to describe their most memorable learning moment in the subject area. They can meet in groups of four and share their stories. Teacher and students listen and ask probing questions. Because it draws on students' memories, this activity usually results in very lively conversations.

In the second stage of the learning cycle, teachers ask students to reflect on patterns or principles that might be found in their observations. This stage moves students beyond the concrete and asks them to reveal the interpretive framework that they currently use. They might, for example, be asked to make a list of the qualities that made each of their learning moments memorable. Students highlight qualities such as caring, challenge, excitement, insight, and so on. As students reveal their current beliefs about the subject matter, the teacher is looking for the points where lessons can be connected to their ideas and beliefs.

Stage three is where the teacher introduces appropriate abstract concepts. If the lesson is about grammar, here is where it is explained. If it is about a principle of science, this is when the teacher has students apply it. The trick is for the teacher to have figured out how to link these abstractions to the frameworks developed from the students' reflections. After some small group discussion, the whole class might share ideas. Through this phase, the teacher makes sure that the content is addressed accurately and in adequate depth; yet much of the discussion is driven by the needs of the students to develop a more informed understanding of the topic that is provided by the abstract material.

In the final stage, the teacher asks students to actively explore ways to experiment with their new understanding. How might they apply the set of principles just learned? As students develop possible applications, they fill in the details of their knowledge, giving the teacher opportunities to uncover any misconceptions or missing information. More important, students immediately connect their knowledge to meaningful concerns.

At each stage of this routine, the teacher is in a position to monitor and direct students as they go through a learning cycle. The emphasis is switched from content to student learning, allowing the teacher to respond to the skills and beliefs that students demonstrate. If students are not able to perform one of these steps well, the teacher can choose to spend additional time on skill building activities, knowing that this will improve their understanding of this lesson as well as enhance their abilities in future learning cycles.

Equipped with routines such as this one, democratic teachers can plan, conduct, and evaluate lessons with greater precision than the traditional lesson plans of content-oriented teachers. The structure of learner-centered routines allows the teacher to avoid the inadequacies of the "jellyfish" approach without having to rely on the disconnectedness found in so many "brick wall" classrooms.

A Democratic Direction

Overwhelmed by content-centered visions of teaching, the learning rhythms of democratic educators have been obscured, hidden from many educators. Activities that lead students into meaningful conversations are not magical but designed according to routines and rhythms that knowingly engage people in the learning process. The history of democratic education has generated broad rhythms and specific routines that can be used to create classroom structures that are truly learner-centered. Using them, teachers can deliberately construct classrooms that realize the practical benefits of democratic ideals.

The recent wave of research on teaching and learning is reconfirming what Dewey noted nearly a century ago: educative processes are intimately intertwined with democratic ones. Even as these new reports reach teachers, however, the powerful grip of content-oriented rhythms will continue to shape the relationship between students and teachers and subject matter. The studies will not convince educators of the potential value of democratic education. Rather, the task will be to demonstrate how classrooms organized around the rhythms and routines grounded in natural learning processes make democratic classrooms more practical educational places.

In my experience, the hardest challenge in transforming myself into a democratic teacher was having to abandon the traditional classroom patterns I had unconsciously internalized in my years of schooling. There is a feeling of panic that comes as teachers step away from routines that cover content without a clear alternative. A runner, a dancer, or a musician succeeds because they find the right rhythm to integrate a variety of dynamic factors. Likewise a teacher needs to find the right rhythm to coordinate the work of the classroom.

Democratic educators need to discover and share learner-centered rhythms. They must explain how to plan, guide, and evaluate classrooms using patterns that help students grow. Teachers will only leave behind the rhythms of traditional schooling when they see how democratic, learner-centered rhythms can better solve the dilemmas of the classroom.

Works Cited

Coloroso, Barbara. 1994. *Kids Are Worth It*. New York: Avon Books.

Dewey, John. [1900, 1902] 1990. *The School and Society and The Child and the Curriculum*. Chicago: University of Chicago Press.

Kolb, David. 1984. *Experiential Learning: Experience as the Source of Learning and Development.* Englewood Cliffs, NJ: Prentice-Hall.

O'Connor, Terence. 1997. Higher Education and the Promise of Democracy. Videotaped presentation at the Lilly Conference on College Teaching. Available at http://web.indstate.edu/staff/democrat.html

Schmuck, Richard, and Patricia Schmuck. 1997. *Group Processes in the Classroom.* 7th ed. Dubuque, IA: Brown and Benchmark Publishers.

(Not Doing) Business as Usual

Jeff Haas and students from Downtown Business Magnets High School, Los Angeles Unified School District

Jeff is a high school English teacher living and working in Los Angeles.

As a secondary English teacher, one of my most significant learning experiences occurred in my second year of teaching, my first at this school, which is minutes from City Hall in downtown Los Angeles. Students in my ninth-grade class were reading Elie Weisel's Holocaust memoir *Night*, and most were very excited about the chance to visit the recently opened Museum of Tolerance, a half-hour ride from school. I filled out and submitted the requisite bus request form.

So far, so good. Here was a clear example of a group of learners eager to deepen their understanding of a literary work by taking their learning beyond the classroom. But because our school is a part of the citywide magnet program (in which sites are subject-specific; one attends this school to focus on science, that one for fine arts, and so forth), my application for a bus was refused. The reason I was given was that the trip was not for "magnet-specific" learning. In other words, the school where I teach is the district's business magnet, and so the trip had to be "business-related" for us to get approval.

Being new to the school and the magnet program, this made no sense to me. But I dutifully reported the news to the students. Their response was, simply, one of disbelief. They were asking for the opportunity to learn more about a subject of intense interest to many of them, and they were being told no? This made no sense to them.

And so I asked the students a question, one, I believe, that fundamentally changed the way I teach: "What do *you* want to do?" By turning the problem-solving process over to the students, by inviting them to become active participants in a real dilemma, I learned a powerful lesson. I learned to get out of the way.

They decided to send a formal letter in which they clearly and effectively stated their case for the bus. They sent it, along with my second application for a bus, directly to the superintendent at the magnet office for the Los Angeles Unified School District. All but one student in the class signed the letter. In three days, we had our answer. Bus refused. There was no acknowledgment of the students' letter. No "I'm sorry but . . . ," no recognition of their efforts. Nothing for the students to believe that they had been heard.

This infuriated the students. They felt ignored and disrespected. In other words, many of them felt, it was just business as usual. This is the way we're always treated. Told what to do, told what not to do.

What we can do, what we can't do. But this group of students decided that this was unacceptable.

> This was no longer a matter of getting a field trip, but of us being heard and not being treated like always.
>
> Ricardo Ramirez

The students went into action.

> And at that moment we knew what we had to do. We got together in class and had a meeting, we separated into committees. We divided the responsibilities. Since we couldn't get a bus we had to set up a committee that would. We even had one that would contact the media, while the others sent letters to the parents asking for their help. Whatever it took we were going to do it. And we were not going to give up.
>
> Brenda Solorio

By the end of the same class period, the students had created and divided into committees to help solve what they now saw clearly as *their* problem. A third committee went looking for a bus. They found one.

The trip to the Museum of Tolerance was a great success. The students were impressed with, and very moved by, their discoveries. They took the trip very seriously, and had a lot of fun. The discussions in class showed that a great deal of learning and understanding had gone on.

How did the students get their bus? The search committee decided, rather on a lark, to go upstairs to our small physical education department, and ask the P.E. teachers if we could borrow their designated bus. No activities were planned for the day of the museum trip; the class had its transportation secured by the next morning. Many students were amused by the fact that they had to go so short a distance to get results, but felt no small satisfaction in overcoming what was for them, indeed, business as usual.

> We were tired of them telling us what we could and couldn't do, simply because they thought we were irresponsible and easily beaten. But we proved them wrong. We refused to accept the usual.
>
> Brenda Solorio

When I say it was important that I learned to get out of the way, I don't mean to make light of such a notion. At the very least, it reinforced something I had intuitively been trying to uncover in my own practice since I had begun teaching; one of my preservice goals was to begin to examine the rigid hierarchies so firmly cemented into our everyday lives on the job. This particular notion of rethinking business as usual was important for me—to put something powerful like this on the table, and to do it for the students. For the students. Wrong.

Students are fully capable of bringing their own issues and concerns to the table. The students didn't need me to do it for them. They needed to be heard. They needed to be given the space to act and speak for themselves. I didn't invite them to write their letter, any more than I was the one who sent them upstairs on their quest. I listened, I asked questions, and I got out of the way. Some of their efforts succeeded, some didn't. That's learning.

The students talked with and listened to each other. They brainstormed, problem-posed, and problem-solved. They learned a little more perhaps about trust and responsibility and working toward something that mattered to them. They addressed an authentic audience.

This was the students' effort to be heard, to declare that they had a stake in their own educations. So obvious it sounds silly to utter. It was their effort to give voice to so much of what they felt about school and the way they have been treated, regarded, situated, named. When I look back on this episode, I see an important piece of my teaching practice settling into place.

School, whether we choose to make it so or not, is fundamentally a place where we teach values. Consciously and unconsciously, we are giving students our take on the world through the things we say and don't say, questions we ask and don't ask, how we listen, and all the other "tools" we bring to the job. It is, I often think, the lessons of the hidden curriculum that are taught best. What is, as Hilton Smith asks, the "social significance" of what I teach? How does the teaching of my content area, English and literature, affect or contribute to the lives of my students? Is adherence to the numerous standards I'm handed down enough? The classroom needs to be a place where all learners can question as well as provide answers, and the questions our students have, and are often waiting to ask, are at least as important a part of learning as the answers they produce.

When the students asked me if they could form committees, it wasn't a matter of me trusting the students to do the job, it was more a matter of them trusting me. Trusting me to let them see the effort through to its conclusion. Trusting me to not prematurely end a meaningful endeavor. Trusting me that they could take risks and make mistakes.

I saw it as my obligation to support the students. It was an opportunity for them to discover their many skills like reflecting, questioning, challenging, problem solving, working together (not merely the "cooperative learning" that has been so quickly reified), taking responsible actions—what Terry O'Connor calls the skills of democratic living (see O'Connor in this chapter). I would help them (when they asked for my help), continue to challenge them, and listen. I asked them to think about the quality of their efforts. Quality work: what it is, not to me, but more important, to each student so that they can begin to ask themselves what for them is a job well done.

For me quality teaching is a way of retrieving once-lost pieces of my own educational past: creativity, a sense of belonging, legitimate decision-making opportunities, a sense of purpose and connection. It is about creating with students a space where we can talk, listen, share, argue, reflect; a safe haven where we can make mistakes as well as succeed, admit to struggles as well as discover something valid in ourselves and our work.

A good part of my job (both meanings of *good* apply) is to help a classroom of students discover its own rhythms, settle into its self-prescribed routines for successful learning. Together, the students and I can begin to find what works best for us.

What has become an important and often difficult and infinitely rewarding piece of my teaching since this learning experience has been to observe students as they move beyond merely working together and instead become something greater for each other. As they problem-solve, argue, support each other, find solutions, and share discoveries, my students have taught me that teaching and learning are reciprocal functions of education, which redefines my role as authority and audience.

> *Learn* is not the word; we accomplished what we set our minds to as a class of students. Finding the bus wasn't easy, much less approaching [the superintendent], but we came through. . . . I think being students is important because we not only learn but we also teach.
>
> Rachel Mejia

As facilitator and mentor, my job is to guide, observe, probe, challenge, model, motivate, listen, and also, most important, to help establish—with the students—clearly stated goals that adhere to what I as the teacher see as satisfying the objectives of the course. O'Connor, drawing from Dewey, says competence (theirs and mine) comes of applying ourselves with our new understandings to new situations. But first, he says, the learner-centered teacher must invite every learner into the conversation. Is there a more important action we as teachers can commit to? As O'Connor says, "Discover your students!"

I ask my students, What kind of environment can we create to further our learning? What is learning about? What are your concerns? What, simply, do you want to learn? If I don't ask them, if I make all the decisions myself, I am doing my students a huge disservice. I am distancing them from collected pieces of their learning, their education, and their lives. If I am keeping them from making decisions and solving problems, I may be teaching English literature, but I am simultaneously teaching a seminar called Alienation 101. My complicity in concretizing their passivity makes it a done deal. I am limiting their opportunities for growth, and many of them don't even know it.

In my few years of teaching, I have too often witnessed, having seen or heard, what I would call the ongoing diminishment of students. Too many of us have. That's why giving the students the opportunity to help create and navigate to their own rhythms, through their own routines, is one of the best things I can do. Built on integrity and authenticity, the challenges and satisfactions ("rewards") become intrinsic.

The students taught me a great deal in their efforts: trust, listening, that input was as important as outcome, and that it is not just OK, but important, to challenge and investigate the hierarchies of business as usual.

> This lesson was important to me because when we were told that we weren't getting the bus, I thought, well, we're not going, but I learned that we can make things happen no matter how old we are or who we are going against. . . . I learned that . . . we all have the power to accomplish things. As a student I learned that us li'l people have the power to go against the big people and win.

Cathy Millan

Recently, I read a brochure touting a new high school under construction near downtown Los Angeles and ran across a statement that startled me: "The [new school] will create a learning environment in which every student will, through a career-oriented program, grow to be lifelong learners and competent, productive employees." I read the statement to a class of ninth-grade students. Things got quiet. I read it again and waited. After a few moments, from across the room, a quiet voice said, "That's all?" The others looked over. "That's all they want the students to be, is employees?" The word had never sounded so hollow to me before.

Others joined in. They had a genuine sense, I think, of what was being asked of students their age by those building, literally, a school from the ground up. Ninth graders, debating the goals and objectives of education, of their education.

Brenda's response sums up what authentic learning can mean:

> It made me believe in myself and that I could do whatever I wanted to do. And if we all join together, that we could stand even stronger and go against anything that comes our way. I don't have to let anyone tell me what my "Business" is, because when it comes to life and learning from it, it is my Business!

Work Cited

Weisel, Elie. 1982. *Night*. New York: Bantam.

4

Reflection as a Tool
for Change

Our Invitation

Given the loneliness of our profession, learning to ask yourself questions and challenging yourself to look for appropriate solutions is critical. In this chapter, Cliff Knapp, teachers he has worked with, and their students share their experiences to teach us what reflection is and how it can be used effectively with students of all ages and most critically with ourselves.

Looking Back to Look Ahead:
Planning for Group Reflection in Schools

Clifford E. Knapp

Cliff, a professor of Curriculum & Instruction at Northern Illinois University, teaches courses in outdoor, experiential, and environmental education.

To reflect is to look back over what has been done so as to extract the net meanings which are the capital stock for intelligent dealing with further experiences. It is the heart of intellectual organization and of the disciplined mind.

John Dewey, *Experience and Education*

This chapter addresses what Dewey calls the heart of intellectual organization—the art and science of leading group reflection sessions. The word *reflection* comes from the Latin root *reflectere,* meaning "to bend back" (Knapp 1992, 15). It is an instructional tool for helping students create more meaning from their lessons. In the educational literature, reflection is also known as *debriefing, processing,* or *teaching for transfer.* Once teachers understand the meaning and importance of reflection in the learning process, they are more likely to make time in their crowded schedules to reflect with their students. The purpose of this chapter is to provide teachers with information, structure, and support for planning and conducting improved reflection sessions. Let's begin by listening in on a school-based scenario.

Carmella Smith, a cooperating teacher, and Mike Jones, her student teacher, are discussing next week's lesson for their sixth-grade class. The selected topic is identifying and classifying some rocks and minerals the students will find on the school grounds.

Carmella: Let's see your lesson plan so I know how you will approach the topic.

Mike: Sure, here it is. I plan to take the students outside to teach about identifying and classifying rocks and minerals. I know there are plenty of rocks and minerals on the school grounds and I think they will enjoy this activity and learn something too.

Carmella: What are your intended student outcomes?

Mike: I heard you say, intended outcomes. Well, I realize that the objectives I set for students don't always materialize. Even if they do, students usually learn others things too. First, I want them to be able to classify what they find by using at least three different characteristics. Then, I want them to identify three of the most commonly found rocks and minerals—sandstone, limestone, and quartz—using a simple dichotomous key. I'd also like them to be able to describe some differences between a rock and a mineral. They've been excited about this topic ever since we went to the geology museum in Mr. Welch's basement.

Carmella: So, your *know-that* kind of knowledge objectives are defining the terms *rock, mineral, sandstone, limestone,* and *quartz.* Your other objectives deal with the *know-how* type of knowledge—the skills of classifying and using an identification key. Right?

Mike: Yes, those are the main ones.

Carmella: How will you find out if they achieve these objectives?

Mike: I'll know if I'm successful because my assessment calls for them to prepare labeled specimens to share with first graders in a few weeks. I'll also test them by asking them to classify a different set of rocks and minerals to see if they can apply these skills to new specimens.

Carmella: You have selected clear objectives and your assessment plan seems logically connected to them. How will you help your students reflect on these experiences afterward? Remember, there is a time lapse of several weeks between their outdoor activities and the final assessments.

Mike: Do you mean that reflecting is different from assessing them on the main objectives of the lesson?

Carmella: Well, it can be. Think of a reflection technique as holding a mirror to a recently completed event. The mirror bends back the light rays or components of the activity so that students can examine what took place. Mirrors are useful tools to help us see things from different vantage points. Looking back over a lesson allows students to review what took place, expand conceptual meanings, fill in cognitive gaps, clear up confusions, or make generalizations and applications for later use.

Reflection can also occur in groups. When students participate together in reflection and verbalize their thoughts and feelings, everyone benefits from what and how they learned. As teachers, we really have broader lesson objectives embedded in the so-called hidden curriculum. For example, your lesson involves going outside in teams of three. I know you want them to work cooperatively and treat each other with respect, but you didn't list these as objectives.

Mike: That's true. Do I have to write those objectives too?

Carmella: No, not really, unless you think you'll lose sight of these while you're teaching. When you think about it, there are many other objectives we hope to achieve by doing these activities. I think you also want students to feel good about themselves and what they accomplish, don't you?

Mike: Sure. I never thought much about those other objectives that lie beneath the surface of every lesson.

Carmella: You may also want them to understand how this lesson applies to the life of scientists and to their own lives as nonscientists. In other words, you want them to know why they should classify and identify things and when these skills are appropriate to use.

Mike: You're right. What else is important to check out?

Carmella: You said that you thought the students would enjoy working together outside. I'm guessing you are concerned with how they feel about the rocks and minerals activity. When we enjoy learning something, we usually want to know more about it and often remember it longer.

Mike: Yes, that's true. I get it! I can ask students to reflect to expand and clarify their attitudes and values about the topic. That can help me know what to do next.

Carmella: The group reflection segments of a lesson usually relate to more than just the stated objectives. Just as indigenous people's stories have several layers of meaning, reflection can help students dig deeper into the lesson. You can help them reflect on their concept or skill attainment, but that's what assessments usually address. They can also examine the process of getting to that knowledge. This is sometimes called *metacognition,* or thinking about thinking. When students verbally share their insights after reviewing and analyzing an event, they can teach each other.

Mike: Now I understand what you mean. In my university methods classes no one talked much about the importance of reflection or showed us how to plan for it. I was challenged to be a reflective practitioner by examining what I do as a teacher, but my professors didn't show me how to use that skill with students. How can I build reflection sessions into my lesson plan?

Carmella: Teaching is part art and part science. There are many variables and unfortunately you don't have control over all of them. However, the more you know about the lesson topic, the learning environment, and the students, the better you can anticipate some areas for reflection. Observing student response to the lesson is very important. One way to help students reflect on their experiences is to prepare some questions beforehand and ask them at appropriate times.

Mike: How will I know the right questions to ask and when to ask them? Are there any steps to follow or recommended guidelines for planning reflection?

Carmella: I usually think about the components of good teaching and what research says about how the human brain works. Constructivist theory suggests that students form new meanings from their past knowledge and experiences by filtering new events through their special ways of viewing the world. Discovering what students know about the topic can guide the reflection process.

Think about helping students elaborate on the main objectives by using higher-order thinking skills such as analyzing, evaluating, applying, or synthesizing. You could ask questions like "How do different grocery stores classify foods?" or "How would identifying rocks and minerals be helpful on a family vacation?" Try to promote critical thinking by digging deeper into the layers below the stated lesson objectives to help them relate the topic to their lives.

Mike: Are there any benefits to leading group reflection during activities or is it better after completing various activities?

Carmella: Conducting a reflection session during or after experiences is appropriate. It's a good idea to provide time at different points in the lesson, always being explicit about what you are doing and why you are doing it.

Mike: So how can reflecting about classifying move us forward?

Carmella: Reflection can clarify the thought process and show how students arrive at answers to the problems you pose. It can help them think about how they reason. Research shows that experts, like geologists, can assist novices, like our students, by explaining out loud how they arrive at particular solutions. In next week's lesson, for example, student teams could diagram and verbally explain how they classified their specimens. I like to teach my students how to lead parts of a reflection session. This takes time, but once students understand how to reflect, they can assist their classmates in the process. Of course, I'm there to support them whenever possible.

Mike: Could reflection also help me discover how individuals become engaged with a lesson?

Carmella: That's possible. How could you design a series of questions that could reveal that?

Mike: Well, I could get some clues by asking students to respond to questions that probe their feelings about different parts of the lesson. I realize that some students want to know how the lesson relates to their lives, so I could ask "What other things have you classified before?" Others are hungry for new facts from books, me, or other sources, so I could ask "What were the most interesting facts you learned about rocks and minerals?" Others want to get involved in hands-on activities like collecting, so I could ask "Which characteristic was best to use in classifying the rocks and minerals?" Others want to apply what they learn to new situations, so I could ask "Could you create your own dichotomous key to identify other rocks and minerals in your collection?" By finding out which parts of the lesson they responded to, I can better understand how they learn.

Carmella: How would you evaluate how they worked together as a team?

Mike: I could ask them to rate their level of teamwork on a numbered scale from one to five, based on how they thought they cooperated. Then I could ask them to make suggestions for improving their cooperation skills. Would that work?

Carmella: Sure. Now you realize you don't always have to ask questions to uncover those deeper levels of the lesson. How would you help the students examine how they feel about themselves?

Mike: As I understand it, intrapersonal skills deal in part with getting in touch with your feelings. I could plan a reflection session to find out how closely they identified with the lesson. I could ask "How many of you might like to become geologists some day?" or "What part of the lesson helped you feel successful? . . . happy? or . . . curious?"

Carmella: You need to decide which of these deeper-level objectives or personal and interpersonal issues you might explore. Also, try to remain flexible because you can always lead a spontaneous reflection session when the right opportunity arises. I remember once when my students were working in coed groups on a contour mapping project. All the boys took over the plane tables and sighting rods before the girls had a chance. I decided to delay the mapping exercise long enough to reflect on the issues of gender sensitivity and empathy for others. Keep in mind that there are many human relations issues that can be addressed directly in context, including expressing appropriate feelings, judging others, listening, leading, following, making group decisions, trusting each other, and respecting human similarities and differences.

If you look for opportunities to deal with these issues, you can help students grow as human beings through reflection. Examine your lesson plan and decide what experiences are worth reflecting on and how you will design the reflection strategy. There are many other ways to structure reflection sessions, but I prefer asking questions. Asking the right question at the right time can be a powerful reflection tool.

Mike: Have we discussed the most important elements in planning reflection sessions?

Carmella: Helping students reflect is not something you can learn in one session. You can't reduce it to a simple formula. It takes practice to feel confident. I just started slowly and experimented with different reflection techniques. Oh, we did leave out one big area in our discussion. We haven't talked about creating a classroom climate in which reflection is most effective.

Mike: That's another thing we didn't learn much about at the university.

Carmella: Whole courses and workshops are devoted to this topic. In fact, counselors, management consultants, and educational psychologists earn degrees before they feel qualified to build effective communities of learners. I find it best to start slowly and try to avoid getting involved too soon in heavy emotional issues. That's the guidance counselor's or school psychologist's job. Always try to keep the depth of the reflection sessions in line with your present level of knowledge and confidence.

Mike: I've seen you discuss norms with your students that address how students will work together. That is a reflective process too.

Carmella: You can examine the positive and negative class norms that affect how students interact. Each norm contributes to or detracts from a sense of community. People usually follow group norms without being aware of them. By making them more explicit and linking them to the group climate, they can influence student behavior. "Enabling" norms such as exchanging genuine compliments, showing caring and acceptance, expressing thoughts and feelings honestly, and respecting individual privacy and differences can facilitate the process of group reflection. If the students don't feel comfortable in the group, they won't say what they really think and feel. The recent trend toward greater awareness of social and emotional learning in schools is long overdue. We need to be concerned with all aspects of our students' lives, not just their cognitive abilities.

Mike: I realize I need to learn more about how to lead reflection sessions. I feel a bit overwhelmed by what I don't know, but I'm willing to try. It seems that reflection can be helpful for all classroom activity, not just the academics.

Carmella: You have already shown that you value reflection as a teaching and learning tool and are using it in your own teaching. That's an important first step.

During this conversation, it became clear that Mike was interested in beginning to explore the idea of leading reflection sessions. Even though he was bright, dedicated to the profession, and skilled in some aspects of teaching, he needed guidance from his cooperating teacher. He wanted to know:

1. How reflection related to the stated objectives and the assessment plan.

2. What other kinds of objectives and individual and group issues could guide reflection and whether or not he should write them into his lesson.

3. How he could build more reflection sessions into his lessons.

4. How to ask the right reflection questions at the right time.

5. Whether there were any guidelines or sequential steps to follow in planning the reflection sessions.

6. Some benefits of leading group reflection, for himself and his students.

7. What reflection techniques could be used in addition to questioning.

8. How to improve the classroom climate so that reflection could be conducted more effectively.

The following guidelines may be helpful to Mike and others as they begin to lead reflection sessions:

1. Begin slowly and keep the reflection sessions short at first.

2. Select appropriate objectives and issues that you are qualified to reflect on with students.

3. Share these objectives and issues openly with the group when appropriate.

4. Allow adequate time for the activities and for reflecting on them.

5. Discuss the supportive or enabling norms and behavior necessary for the group to function more effectively.

6. Respect the students' rights to remain silent or to "pass" during the reflection sessions; consider keeping some information confidential within the group.

7. Respond to students in ways that enhance their self-esteem, build their confidence, and maintain their comfort levels in the group.

8. Provide opportunities for all students to meet their needs by using their special strengths and intelligences.

9. Continually learn more about psychology, communications, and group dynamics through involvement with support groups, readings, lectures, and courses.

10. Always remain flexible and open to changes in the focus of the lesson.

Students need to learn how to reflect by themselves and in groups. One way to achieve this goal is to guide them through the process together. Students can improve their reasoning, problem solving, and critical thinking abilities by discussing them openly. They can become more aware of their learning preferences and how they feel about the lessons. Reflection sessions can reveal, expand, and clarify concepts and skills related to the planned and unplanned curriculum. They can also help students analyze the group's social dynamics while learning about norms related to trust, caring, safety, and other human relations goals. Students can investigate relationships between the lessons and their personal interests, competencies, and values. Reflection can also help students transfer school-learned knowledge to their lives outside of school and bring greater meaning to the curriculum. It can also help them identify and focus on the big ideas of the lessons and connect the separate components to larger wholes. Finally, reflection can assist students in making better sense of their lessons and in gaining deeper understanding of the purpose for schooling, now and in the future.

Learning how to plan and implement reflection sessions is a challenge for all teachers. If they are willing to accept this challenge, Dewey's view that reflection is the heart of intellectual organization and of the disciplined mind will be realized.

Works Cited

Dewey, John. 1938. *Experience and Education.* New York: Collier Books.

Knapp, C. 1992. *Lasting Lessons: A Teacher's Guide to Reflecting on Experience.* Charleston, WV: ERIC Clearinghouse on Rural Education and Small Schools.

Reflecting on Reflection

Kim Douillard, Jan Hamilton, and their students, Cardiff-by-the-Sea

Kim and Jan teach for the Cardiff School District in Cardiff-by-the-Sea, California. For the past four years they have been collaborating and coteaching a first-, second-, and third-grade multiage class that they created.

Reflection seems easy to explain—you know, it's like looking in a mirror. But no, that isn't it at all. Reflection is more like looking into water. Each time you look, you see something a little different. Everything affects the reflection; light, wind, currents, rocks, angles, and the life within the water. Of course, reflection is also affected by the individual, who sometimes looks closely and at other times takes a broader view. Through reflection we can look deep inside or stay on the surface.

Reflecting with students is a challenge. Effective reflection requires a safe environment. Students need to be secure and comfortable to share what they know, think, and feel honestly. By setting the tone and asking the right questions teachers can get reflections filled with insight and wonder. And the more students practice reflection the better they get. This is true for the teachers as well.

Reflection takes time, time to learn how to reflect well and the time to pull loose ends together at the conclusion of a lesson. It is also time that is well spent. Students become more engaged and excited as they gather the threads of a lesson or observation. Verbal reflection takes on a sense of urgency, a desire to share a new connection or pose a question. Written reflection prompts writing that shows rather than tells what is taking place in the learner's mind.

Reflecting takes learning to a different level. It takes the facts and information and merges them with personal connections, the world at large and all we already know. It connects new learning to previous learning, allowing for easier retrieval. We make discoveries as we reflect, letting our learning lead us down new paths. When we reflect, our learning takes different shapes and continues to grow.

During our study of the forest our students wrote these reflections:

I think it was neat going under the canopy of branches and leaves. It reminded me about the kelp forest with the canopy we were studying before.

Keiko Iida, third grader

I learned something from the tree also, that there are different kinds of trees, not just the one that is in your head, because a pepper tree had never come to my mind before. The tree is still a mystery to me, though. There is much more for me to discover. I just haven't discovered it yet!

Joanna Poceta, second grader

This tree was not as tall as I had remembered it from times I did not mean to look at it.

Janaki Jagannath, third grader

The more I looked the more I discovered about the tree. And as I discovered more about the tree I learned I was relating to nature. And I was crafting a whole new tree inside my head.

Taylor Eaton, third grader

When I went out to look at a tree and I thought I knew all about trees, of course when I went out there were many things I didn't know about trees.

Sierra French, first grader

During our Families and Science Together (FAST) Day, we asked parents to reflect on the experience of learning with their child:

What this day has done is join together my son's thirst for new knowledge and my search for lost thoughts, and hopefully we can join together and have fun finding them both.

Jay Kutlow

I think working with the kids makes us look at things on a different level. Some say it's a simple or basic level, but we as adults sometimes are so complex that we miss the basics, therefore missing the bigger picture.

Kim Morris

Taking a sapling together and preparing it with soil and water, while watching his brown hand against mine against the soil, caused me to recognize our relation to nature and all living things. The experience was at once metaphorical and magical.

Mario Chacon

When we take the time to reflect, we no longer look at things the same way. A new perspective of awe, wonder, and an occasional "aha" takes place. While we know that deeper learning is the result of reflection, we wanted to learn more about how our students did reflections and what they thought about them. Together we brainstormed their perception of reflection. The responses from our first, second, and third graders were: reflection is reviewing, connecting, thinking back and explaining, describing, telling what you learned and what you already know, searching your mind for old things, and telling what you feel. At the conclusion of this discussion we posed these questions to our students: How do you do reflections? What do you think about them? After reflecting on reflection, our students gave us some insight into their thinking:

> When I do a reflection, to me it's like I'm a camera. When I reflect, the picture develops in my mind and then I describe the picture.
>
> Keiko Iida

> To do a reflection is thinking about what you remember. I think what makes it easier is if you have a lot of experience. I think what makes it harder is if you're in first grade and you haven't had that much experience.
>
> Ryan Morris, first grader

> When I write a reflection, I always think back and explain. I know when I am writing a good reflection, when I fall into my paper. I wish that happened all the time!
>
> Janaki Jagannath

> It makes it harder when they say, "Reflect on this." It's a lot funner when the teacher explains it well. When she talks about it a little while before we reflect.
>
> Zachary Kutlow, second grader

Though reflecting often occurs naturally, almost without thinking, bringing reflection to the surface—being aware of your own thought processes—takes some effort. We have found that oral reflections are the easiest and most effective way to begin. Students begin with the concrete, simply stating what they did. This concrete beginning offers a risk-free entrance into the reflection process. This is the point where a teacher's use of careful, open-ended questions can broaden a simple review into an effective reflection session. We must be vigilant to avoid falling into the "correct answer" frame of mind. We have to let our students know that we value their thinking rather than "fishing" for that perfect response. We also find that their responses open the frame of reference for the entire class and take us in directions that we might not have imagined.

Our students often remind us that reflection takes practice. It is essential to reflect regularly and to allow adequate time for the process.

Students are often unaware that they are reflecting. By building time into the school day for reflection and "thinking about thinking" students become more aware of their learning and consciously make connections to their own experience. Reflection, as a regular part of our routine, deepens the learning experience for learners of all ages.

5

Creating a Community and Building Trust

Our Invitation

Creating a community in your classroom where students learn to trust themselves, each other, and you to make decisions together and choose responsible behavior is a goal that can be achieved. Chapter 5 shows you ways to begin to engage students in nonthreatening activities where they can learn to listen to each other and be successful with group problem posing and solving. More children's voices will help you see their points of view about why these practices are powerful tools for moving toward an active, caring classroom. Antonio Pessegueiro's essay will challenge you to consider ways in which schools could include team building in the curriculum.

How to Create a Community

J. Cynthia McDermott, Cliff Knapp, and Sharon Setoguchi

What does it mean to build a community of learners? How do we create communities that are democratic? What examples have you participated in or seen? Westheimer and Kahne (1993, 325) state that "researchers have found that teacher behavior . . . often reflects the emphasis on individualism and autonomy so pervasive in our culture." If that's true, creating community is a practice that could be unpopular and difficult. Place on top of this the coercive, compulsory nature of the classroom and school, and it is no wonder so few models exist.

So why would we encourage teachers to work with students to deliberately change the paradigm of the classroom? Ralph Peterson (1992) writes that creating a caring community means that all members can safely work together to solve problems and investigate their world. Peterson describes an image that is difficult to forget. Teacher and students live their lives during the day in a room the size of most American living rooms. (Imagine inviting thirty children to spend the day in *your* living room!) What skills do we all need to make that experience wholesome?

It might be interesting to look at one clearly articulated model of community before we look at what happens in schools.

M. Scott Peck (1987) outlines four steps that most deliberately formed groups follow. Groups usually start with pseudocommunity, a false acceptance of others involving role playing and mask wearing. He realized that groups take time and effort to form, so starting this way is to be expected. In pseudocommunity, conflict is usually avoided rather than dealt with directly. The next step is usually chaos. This step centers around well-intentioned attempts to heal and convert each other to one way of thinking. Most groups need this stage of struggle and confusion in order to move on. It is marked by advice giving, arguing, and adhering to one's own views. At this often painful stage, few problems are solved and little sense of community is felt. The third step is emptiness. It is a way of escaping chaos and making the transition to community. This stage involves emptying personal barriers to communication such as negative feelings, false assumptions, or unaccepting behaviors. Preconceived notions about members of the group can prevent people from hearing each other. Our need to control, heal, convert, or manipulate others can be a barrier to achieving community.

At the final stage, true community, the group can begin to work on real projects. If attention is not paid to maintaining the community over time, it may revert to earlier stages. There are significant parallels to the stages of community and the integration of the individual. JoAnne

Ishimine's chapter describes this connection well. Peck realized that communities must be inclusive and that human differences should be celebrated as gifts. Group members should commit to coexistence and strive for consensus in decision making. They should speak out for what they believe and at the same time listen to what others are saying, striving to develop a climate of safety.

In order for democracy to thrive in a classroom (or anywhere else for that matter), a group must learn the foundational social skills necessary so that authentic conversations can take place. This requires shared experiences that can form the basis for the discussion and development of three key elements: trust, risk taking, and cooperation. Of course, this sounds exciting and wonderful, but classrooms are not deliberately formed by the students and the teachers. Our classrooms are created out of chaos and accident, and unfortunately the composition changes frequently as children move in and out of districts. We do not have the advantages that a deliberately formed and stable community has.

Creating democracy requires a comprehensive set of practices that go far beyond a few cooperative lessons and tricks. Developing a classroom community will not take place quickly, nor will it take place in a series of neat and tidy steps. There is no cookbook that gives the ingredients and procedures resulting in a final product. The process must be undertaken deliberately and with the students as full participants. The results of creating a team feeling, of moving together to enhance learning are well articulated by Antonio Pessegueiro in the next section.

Building a democratic community of learners in a compulsory and authoritarian environment such as a school where many elements for success—the willingness to come together voluntarily, particularly to challenge the status quo; having authentic problems to pose and solve; the ability to actively listen to ourselves and others; time and consistent effort; and practice in working collaboratively and risk taking— are often missing is a formidable task. But there are specific social skills that can be used that will provide the shared experiences needed to help a classroom grow as a community, albeit pseudo at first.

Group Challenges

First, the class needs group challenges such as the following example. Let your class know that you will give this direction only once, then say "Please stand (or sit) in groups according to your birthday months." Observe and note the skills they are using to complete the task. When the task is complete, ask them to tell you what skills they used. List them on a piece of chart paper to be added to later. Challenges exist on a continuum and involve emotional, physical, and cognitive skills.

Each challenge provides a new level of risk for each individual and the group as a whole.

Dave Nettell, an educational consultant, shares his skills about how to handle a challenge. "During the time that your group is working on this birthday challenge, practice keeping your mouth, facial expressions, and body language in check. Pay attention to how often the students look to you for clues and the assurance that they're doing it 'the right way.' You will undoubtedly be asked questions about how to do it. Most, if not all of them, are programmed (consciously or unconsciously) to have you repeat the direction. 'If I answer that question, I'll be repeating the direction, right?' is one of the responses I use most often. Another remark I make is 'If I answer your questions, I'll be helping you with this challenge. I'm interested in how you do it— not how you and I do it together. You know, the only way people ever get good at making decisions and working together is by doing it' " (1996, 25).

It is important to remember that the more authentic the problem, the more closely the group will come to building a real community. But created or contrived challenges are helpful and appropriate ways to introduce working together in a class.

Noncompetitive Group Challenges

The second issue is that these challenges need to be noncompetitive. The birthday challenge could be made competitive by dividing the class in two and asking them to decide which side can do the challenge fastest. As Alfie Kohn so clearly explains in *No Contest* (1986), competition creates distrust, an oppositional response and norm to building community. The challenges must be about problem posing and solving. The participants must be trusted to develop the solutions and to take risks in their implementation. The teacher's role is primarily to assure the physical and emotional safety of everyone. Central to this process is a recognition that there is no one right way to solve the problem. Many possibilities are acceptable. Because these challenges are usually fun, allow students choices, create opportunities for everyone to talk and be listened to, and create a sense of belonging to the group, they are need satisfying. (See J. Cynthia McDermott's chapter.)

Active Listening

Listening is the key to creating caring relationships. So how do you teach this skill? If a class has trouble listening to one another, the prospect of creating a democratic community is threatened. First, practice listening by really listening to your class. Gordon's active listening skills and I-messages (see JoAnne Ishimine's chapter) are extremely helpful in this area of skill development. What are the ways in which you convince students that you're listening to them? What are the ways that you know they are listening to you and to each other? Sit down with your class and ask them about listening. What is listening? What is excellent listening? What does it look like, sound like, and feel like? How do you know someone is really listening to you? How can you convince someone you are really listening to them? Who are examples of good listeners? Why do some people get listened to more or better than others?

Start giving your directions only once and expect excellent listening. Encourage the students to work together and share information when someone misses a direction. Continue to model excellent listening yourself. Continue giving them cooperative challenges. For example, "Sit in groups according to your favorite fruit." "Line up in alphabetical order." Do this three to four times a day, every day. Mistakes = information is an important equation to keep in mind when doing cooperative challenges, especially those that are more complicated and take more community building skills.

Risk Taking

A fourth element relates to risk. Challenges can help level the playing field because they provide different learners with different kinds of stages on which to demonstrate competence. A nonverbal student may do very well at problem posing, for example. But emotional and physical safety is extremely important if the classroom is to be a safe and supportive environment. A powerful tool that can increase this is the act of passing, or opting out of participation temporarily. Again Nettell says, "The participants right (and responsibility to both themselves and the rest of the group) to decide when, where, and how to challenge themselves is part of the foundation laid before the group attempts any challenge. The actual act of passing is usually a public statement, though it sometimes can be a communication between the individual and the facilitator. No one should ever be forced, either overtly or tacitly, to attempt or to complete any challenge" (1996, 39). Passing is a respectful tool that allows participants to move at their own rate.

Sensitive Debriefing

The fifth condition is careful and sensitive reflection or debriefing. This is necessary so that the process (not the product—completion of the challenge) is highlighted. It does not need to be done after every challenge nor does it have to be done with the whole group. Reflecting is an important way to engage in practice, and Cliff Knapp in Chapter 4 provides skills helpful in this area.

If we look at a true community experiment, such as the creation of Hull House in Chicago by Jane Addams, we can see the significant possibilities of teamwork clearly. Addams believed that the poverty and pessimism of the Chicago slums in 1889 was unacceptable. Lack of jobs, sanitary conditions, and schooling were a few of the problems she felt needed to be changed. She set about creating a place where problems could be collectively solved in a "salon" of democracy, as it came to be called. Hull House exemplified a community, a place where individuals could practice what John Dewey supported—advancing the skills necessary to sustain a democratic society.

Dewey and Addams and many others have clearly written about these skills. A democratic community needs members who care about themselves and are altruistic, who have problem posing and solving skills, who attempt to live an integrated life, who are conscientious and are good neighbors. A community functions well when these skills are practiced.

Compulsory education with mandated curricula can be a significant obstacle to building a community in a school or a classroom. Everyone is there because of laws and sanctions and the system's rules and regulations punish individuals who challenge the status quo. If schools were engaged in preparing children for future engagement as active participants in a democratic process, then creating a community of learners would not be an unusual act, as it is now. As your community culture develops, you can support and extend it by developing and encouraging rituals, rites, and ceremonies that honor the participants. Challenge your students to develop these together. Through it all, however, practice, reflection, and trusting students will create unlimited community possibilities.

Works Cited

Kohn, A. 1986. *No Contest—The Case Against Competition: Why We Lose in Our Race to Win.* Boston: Houghton Mifflin.

Nettell, D. 1996. *Cooperative Adventures Teacher's Handbook.* Sausalito, CA: Cooperative Adventures.

Peck, M. S. 1987. *The Different Drum: Community-making and Peace.* New York: Simon and Schuster.

Peterson, R. 1992. *Life in a Crowded Place: Making a Learning Community.* Portsmouth, NH: Heinemann.

Westheimer, J., and J. Kahne. 1993. "Building School Communities: An Experience-based Model." *Phi Delta Kappan* 75: 324–28.

Team Building

Antonio Pessegueiro

Antonio Pessegueiro is a senior at Carson High School, Los Angeles Unified School District.

As students begin their teenage years, their friends and social status tend to guide their lives. Whether it is being in touch with the latest fashions or being knowledgeable of the current lingo, students continually desire to fit in. Fear of being labeled an outsider is a teenager's nightmare.

Team-building activities in the classroom can be the connection between a classroom education and a student's social life in and outside of school. The relationship shared by those in a peer group needs to be similar to the one shared by those in a classroom community. Team-building activities develop several important social skills that help the group improve their problem-solving skills: speaking up, honoring your commitments, giving and asking for feedback, respecting others, practicing good communication, and developing trust.

Speaking Up

Speaking up means sharing one's personal opinions, observations, and feelings—limiting yourself to "I . . ." statements. The individual is important to the team. Expressing what is on a person's mind is important to the success of the team. Students cannot learn from each other unless they themselves open up and speak out. In a group that has become a team, students can easily say what is on their minds, how they feel, and what their opinions on the task at hand may be.

Honoring Your Commitment

The process is often as important as the product that the team is trying to produce. Each student needs to commit to the team. Empty commitments are common in the life of a teenager. Last-minute, spontaneous decisions may render the long-term commitments of a teen useless. However, young people will commit to something they deem important. If students care about the success of their team or their group, students will be less likely to renege on their commitments. Learning to commit to the process is an important part of team-building activities.

Giving and Asking for Feedback

Clearing the air by openly discussing problems and concerns may be difficult, but such openness can help to move the group forward. For a group to function well as a team, questions and concerns of the group need to be easily and openly discussed. The wide array of experiences that are available to any classroom group can help a group explore all the facets of a given topic or problem presented to them. Teamwork requires that a group be able to learn from each other and themselves by asking questions and responding to each other.

Respecting Others

People have a right to feel whatever it is they feel; and to the best of their ability, they should attempt to be nonjudgmental toward others. This is one of the most important skills learned in team-building activities. Respect is necessary in a team. The different characteristics and backgrounds represented in most groups require that each member respect the others for who they are, what they do, and how they do it. Team-building activities allow students with different strengths to shine at different times. This allows team members to learn to respect these differences.

Practicing Good Communication Skills

Teamwork requires the participation of everyone. A person can often contribute by listening and building on the ideas of others. Communication is the key to all team-building activities. Students tend to develop their own lingo and function better when they are around others who share the same language. The basis for this lies in the students' abilities to understand each other and to communicate effectively. Shared experiences help the students to develop their communication skills.

Developing Trust

Acts such as nay-saying, taking cheap shots, making attacks, arguing to win, or withholding information can impede team effectiveness. When you are depending on the actions and commitments of those in your group, trust between members is essential. Learning to work with others and to trust them completely is an important goal of team-building activities.

The idea of team building is very important in school. As teens enter high school, style and social status become the high points of their school experience. This mentality should continue in the classroom. Without a sense of community or a well-functioning team, sharing knowledge is difficult, if not impossible. Learning to work with others in a noncompetitive atmosphere makes approaching a difficult math problem or interpreting poetry or literature easier. The wide array of knowledge and backgrounds available in a diverse group of students makes the learning process more fun for each individual.

Cooperative group learning, where students sit in circles in the classroom rather than rows, has been a popular method of education at Carson High School. Teachers use group work as a tool for developing the talents of the individual and bringing each of those talents together to accomplish a common task. This learning approach helps students achieve more than they would without the benefit of the group. Students learn to work together, solve problems, and support each other much like they do in social situations outside of school.

It's a Matter of Choice

Alma D'Aleo and her first graders from 232nd Street School, Los Angeles Unified School District

Alma comes from an art and business background and has taught in Los Angeles Unified School District for over eleven years.

Creating a democratic classroom is a challenge, and I have often had anxiety about whether I was doing it "right." Teachers are expected to teach in a particular way but the kind of classroom I develop allows for chaos to be part of the process. That is where the creativity comes from, but it is often hard to hold onto that mantra. I want a voice, but that is sometimes difficult. But I trust in the innate ability of children to know good from bad and to believe in fairness. Many classroom and school leaders are focused on control, but in a democratic classroom that concept has to be rethought. I want my students to freely offer whatever they need to discuss. I want my students to have a chance to rethink their decisions and to trust that they will be heard.

I do not consider myself an expert, but I think this is just the right thing to do. Gregory Corso in his poem "Marriage" writes: "How else to be other than I am." Those words describe how I create our classroom climate by providing choices as a legitimate way of pointing children toward social skills and problem solving that will serve them far better than memorizing lessons will. Research demonstrates that the most common reason for losing a job is the inability to work with a group. In our class, we try to be sensitive to others' feelings and ideas. When we work together I see kids who I might not expect to say anything become the problem solvers. Team-building activities allow the hidden specialness to show and to encourage the closet geniuses to come forward. A classroom has to be a loving place where every child is accepted.

I start the day by reviewing the agenda so they know what we will be doing. We work together as partners; I don't spring things on them. The students are privy to everything; we work as much as possible as equals. I trust them as competent people.

After recess is problem-solving time. We set a timer for an agreed-upon time, usually ten minutes, and then students verbally offer their concerns. My group of children are predominantly non-English speakers, and I encourage as much oral language development as possible. One girl may say that the older children are taking her ball on the playground. Others offer suggestions or reminders about other ideas we have generated earlier. The children decide what they want to do. I try not to solve all of their problems, but I will step in if they get stuck. When they say they have a problem, we discuss what we can ask people to do. Since the solutions they come up with are for their problem, they have a vested interest in solving it. As Glasser advises, when we all agree then we follow the plan. We observe, pinpoint the problem, brainstorm solutions, pick one, and then follow it. They all adhere to it in a more persistent and keener way because they own it.

I tell them that in ten years or so they will be voting. Is it ever too early in school to practice democracy? I hear other teachers and parents say that first graders are too young to think for themselves and they need to be told what to do. But as I guide them into seeing the bigger picture, they get it. I am trying to prepare them for life because they will probably never be in another classroom like mine. The students really need social skills of caring and valuing. This classroom is mainly about emotional well-being. I want my students to feel validated. I asked them to contribute to this book and their words follow. Remember that these are students who do not speak English as a first language, yet they were very clear about what matters to them. I asked them to say what they liked and what they did not. They are learning to find their voices.

What I Like

I like making choices. (Jerico Musngi)

I like voting. (Audrey Rodarte-Griffith)

I like to choose the right. (Michael Brown)

I like to choose what I like to choose. (Mark Griego)

What I Don't Like

I don't like being bossed around. (Michael Brown, Andrew Alonzo, Jerico Musngi)

I don't like feeling sad. (Aide Herrera)

Other Comments

Voting makes me healthy. (Amanda Werth)

Choosing makes me smart. (Amy Chavez)

The children have taken ownership of the class. When visitors arrive, they proudly describe how they decided to move their desks into two long lines so that everyone could see. They describe how they solve problems and invite anyone interested to participate in their problem solving. There is constant and productive talk, and they are learning to work with many different kinds of people and to solve their problems by themselves. It is very exciting to see first graders demonstrate the necessary and complex skills of citizenship with such enthusiasm and joy.

6

Teaching from the Heart

Our Invitation

Sometimes the work we do with students requires active listening and an understanding of counseling skills so that students can be heard. Although we can't be counselors, psychologists, or parents to our students, we can learn some counseling skills that will help us be more effective teachers. This chapter, written by JoAnne Ishmine, Sharon Setoguchi, Jeff Haas, and Cynthia McDermott, explains why feelings are important and the skills you need to learn to decide what the problem is, who owns it, and how to work with students to resolve conflicts and talk with students. Sally Gregory and her students add thoughtful responses to these ideas.

Emotions, Conflict, and Their Importance in Educating the Whole Person

JoAnne Ishimine, J. Cynthia McDermott,
Jeff Haas, and Sharon Setoguchi

JoAnne is a marriage and family counselor in the Los Angeles area.

In *Emotional Intelligence* (1995), Daniel Goleman defines E.Q., in part, as having the ability to "motivate oneself and persist in the face of frustrations; to control impulse and delay gratification, to regulate one's moods and keep distress from swamping the ability to think; to empathize and hope" (34). These "crucial emotional competencies can indeed be learned and improved upon by children, if we bother to teach them" (34).

In order to have a meaningful democratic practice, it is necessary to have individuals who have the knowledge and freedom to be true to themselves, who decide what they believe in and speak up for it, and who are able to resolve conflicts with others. Salovey (in Goleman 1995, 43) defines five domains that are important to such abilities: knowing your emotions, managing emotions, motivating yourself, recognizing emotions in others, and handling relationships. Goleman adds,

> The extent to which emotional upsets can interfere with mental life is no news to teachers. Students who are anxious, angry, or depressed don't learn; people who are caught in these states do not take in information efficiently or deal with it well. When emotions overwhelm concentration, what is being swamped is the mental capacity cognitive scientists call "working memory," the ability to hold in mind all information relevant to the task at hand. (78–79)

The model presently used by schools, which focuses on cognition, power, and control, gets in the way of children recognizing and learning to respect their talents, what they want, and what in their lives motivates them to be cooperative, productive citizens. "Emotions out of control impede the intellect. But . . . we can bring out-of-control emotions back into line; this emotional competence is the master aptitude, facilitating all other kinds of intelligence" (Goleman 1995, 86).

How do we know that kids' emotions are not under control? They might show us in any number of ways—by acting out, not talking, not participating, being resistant, being absent, doing poor work, feeling sad or angry, or talking back. Teachers often are unhappy with such responses since most feel that their requests are not unreasonable: come to class, do the work, don't bother anybody, be cooperative and respect-ful. How hard is that? But if Goleman is correct, then much is getting in the way of the kinds of participation we want from our students.

Virginia Satir's counseling perspectives describe the family as a system. Although she does not write about schools per se, many coun-selors would agree that schools and classrooms are very much like a family system, with different members playing different roles at differ-ent times. In general, parents usually want children to be cooperative and respectful. Often they experience or witness the same behaviors as teachers. Why is that? Why can't children just do what they are told?

Part of the answer is that many adults try to get children to do things by using their controlling power. Thomas Gordon created a particularly effective model for understanding this, in which there are four kinds of authority: Authority E, Authority J, Authority C, and Authority P.

The first is Authority E, which any individual has because they are an Expert at something. For example, you may have a child in your class who takes care of the turtle better than anyone else. Considered the expert by others, no one questions the directions they may give about how to feed or clean the turtle.

The second type is Authority J, which is related to the Jobs we do. Teachers have certain authority because they are expected to keep a class safe and well organized. Children expect teachers to have this authority and usually accept it.

Authority C represents those situations where people have come to informal agreements (Commitments and Contracts) about who has which responsibilities. Your daughter always gets the mail when she comes home; your mother always calls on Sunday morning. This is authority granted through an understanding between people and can change when it no longer works.

The last type of authority is the one we see most in schools. Authority P, using control (Power), dominates, coerces, and says, "Do it my way, now!" Also, it both provides rewards for "good" behavior and punishes "bad" behavior. Gordon states, "It seldom hurts an adult-child relationship for the adult to be *authoritative*—Authority J—or to be an *authority* on a subject—Authority E—but it does harm the rela-tionship to be *authoritarian*—Authority P" (17).

What Gordon means by harm is that the trust between the two indi-viduals diminishes. When this happens it becomes increasingly difficult for respect to occur and the problems that arise become more and more difficult to solve. Without understanding the importance of effective relationship skills in creating cooperation, mutual respect, and harmony, problems cannot be accurately defined and resolved without creating resentment, resistance, and a desire to get even or to withdraw participation from the relationship. How power is used in a relationship determines what kind of relationship will result. When someone uses power as control against someone to get what they want, boundary violations, resentment, and revenge are the results. It is healthy to want control of your own life. It is unhealthy to use force to control, coerce, or violate another. Relationships that are successful are based on caring, concern, and trust. Unsuccessful ones are based on power and control.

Classrooms of students who have developed the awareness and skills to consciously integrate their thoughts and feelings can resolve intrapersonal and interpersonal conflicts. Most individuals, however, often feel their needs are not getting met. Their own feelings of frustration, powerlessness, and inadequacy surface and they become defensive, using whatever role they can to cope with the tension, conflict, and unsatisfied needs they are experiencing.

In Satir's work, these roles are described by the way people communicate. We speak with our whole body and often "say" things that are different than what we intend. When we are not feeling loved or trusted, we often choose one of the following survival communication styles: we placate, blame, act super-reasonable, feign irrelevance, or demonstrate congruence.

A Placater says things such as "I'm no good" and "you are better than I am." Placaters do not take care of themselves, recognize their needs, or act to get them met. They sees themselves as victims. The Blamer is a tyrant, often highly critical of others, often an aggressor who feels that they are the center of the universe. The Super-reasonable type, Satir says, is "very useful . . . for school teachers and others who interact with pieces of paper for their livelihood—in which words come out super-reasonable. When this happens, of course, the words bear no relationship to how one feels" (41). Unfortunately, this style depends on cognitive response and usually ignores feelings. The Irrelevance communicator ignores everything that is going on by denying, acting out, or changing the topic. These first four styles, Satir says, "are all understandable, logical outcomes of how people have learned to manage their survival in the presence of stress. . . . Ninety-nine percent of us were brought up on the authority system which says, You are OK if you obey me and if you are like me. . . . I do not see them as anybody's perversions or anybody's deliberate attempts to injure somebody, although they do cause plenty of injury" (48). The Congruence communicator, on the other hand, uses feelings, cognition, and self-respect to say what is felt, what is meant, and also to communicate respect. Unconscious injury to another is far less likely to occur.

An understanding of roles is also vital to the classroom teacher whose intention is to provide an environment conducive to learning. If teachers can recognize that a student's act or role is masking a more serious issue or conflict, they can begin to identify an underlying problem that needs to be addressed and resolved to restore the harmony both in the individual and in the learning environment. This ability requires training and, importantly, practice. Because effective communication and feeling- and problem-identification skills basic to successful relationships are not generally a part of teacher education, teachers are at a real disadvantage when faced with many kinds of conflicts in the classroom setting. They perceive a student's acting out as a personal failure to maintain control or to be a good teacher.

Counselors are trained to listen for feelings and nonverbal body language, and mirroring or reflective listening is central to their goal of assisting people to find accurate words to express inner feelings and conflicts. By their listening, the other person can begin to learn who they really are, what they feel, what they like and don't like, and they can begin to develop the foundation for self-knowledge upon which is built self-discipline and self control.

The good news is this is very possible, if those who at present have the most power in the classroom make an explicit commitment to begin to share the power and use participatory, democratic conflict resolution rather than punishment, power, and control.

In his Effective Communication and Conflict Resolution courses, Thomas Gordon describes three methods people use when confronted with conflict in their lives and relationships. The first two are based on a power and control, win-lose (or no-win) model. The third one is based on the democratic principles of equality and mutual respect.

Method I, or "Dissin," says that people, when confronted with conflict, take a controller's or blamer's stance. The person with the greater power in a relationship (i.e., teacher, principal, parent, policeman, bigger person, wealthier person) "wins" by forcing a solution on the other person. The less powerful one has no say in the solution and ends up resentful.

Method II, or "Letting yourself get dissed," is the victim or placater's stance. The person who has *more* (or at least equal) power or status feels unable to self-disclose or to speak up for their rights, needs, or desires, but instead gives in or withdraws. By doing this their feelings, needs, and perspective are not "invited" as part of the solution. The other "wins." The person who has surrendered, or allowed their boundaries to be violated, or has power stolen from them, still gets resentful. A very common example of this is when a two-year-old in a grocery store acts out at the checkout counter until the parent gives in and buys the candy that the child wants. The child wins, the adult gets resentful, and you can imagine how that impacts their relationship.

Gordon's Method III is "No-Lose Conflict Resolution." When two individuals—whether of equal or unequal power—have a conflict, they use the skills of reflective listening, nonblaming, nonattacking self-disclosure, and an empathic "shifting of gears" from self-disclosure to reflective listening when resistance arises, to define their conflict clearly in terms of the needs and feelings of both people. In an atmosphere of mutual respect the two people work together to create a solution that will meet the needs, feelings, values, and goals of both. When a solution that is acceptable is created, both end up with a sense of being heard, valued, respected, cared about, and satisfied. No one loses, no one is resentful, and there is no need or desire for retaliation, getting even, or saving face.

Practical, as well as meaningful, skills can be learned and used to facilitate no-lose conflict resolution. It is important to help students learn these skills as well for them to become active participants in choosing healthy ways to interact and build relationships. These include identifying feelings, perception and empathy development, problem posing and solving, reflective listening, and avoiding roadblocks to communication.

Identifying Feelings

William Glasser says that caring is listening. It is important that teachers learn to be comfortable with the expression of a student's feelings, as well as to have the skills and courage to identify and self-disclose their own when there is a conflict between teacher and student. Many students have an innate talent for self-expression found more through drawing, music, movement, and drama than in verbal expression, but since classrooms focus predominantly on the cognitive, verbal expression skills, it is vital to help students find accurate (or even approximate) words to express their feelings. Asking students to think about how they feel about the work they are doing and modeling these expressions can begin to create a space where feelings are discussed honestly.

Perception and Empathy

Another area where misunderstanding and lack of knowledge leads to power struggles is in the area of perception. Conflicts often arise in a relationship when someone attempts to impose their personal worldview on someone else. Figure 6–1 can be used as an illustration of how one event, circumstance, scene, or situation can look one way to one person and totally different to another. What do you see? Is it a young woman? An old witch? An eagle? If someone approaches an open-ended choice such as this with an assertion of power and control, they will by necessity deny another person's viewpoint that they do not

Figure 6–1

agree with and may accuse the other of being either ignorant, crazy, or lying, but most certainly wrong. If the intent is to defend one's position as right, a power struggle or violence can erupt.

If, on the other hand, the intention is to learn and understand something about the other person's point of view, this difference of perspective will lead both to broaden their points of view. Using this enigmatic illustration, ask students to compare what they see. Students often move from the initial struggle over the certainty that they are right to a lively excitement and joy as they discover, by sharing points of view, that there is much more to behold in the picture than a limited perspective allows. An attitude of being right and forcing someone to see it one way is that of power and control. An attitude of mutual respect, based on an intention to learn from each other creates a varied, interesting, and joyful world.

Problem Posing and Solving

Another problem occurs when a one-sided solution precedes an understanding of the real problem. People often go into battle over whose solution is to be accepted without ever accurately defining the problem. This phenomenon doesn't happen out of willful spite as much as out of ignorance of the core feelings and unsatisfied needs that underlie most conflicts and the lack of vocabulary to express the feelings. Instead of recognizing that the conflict is based on an unsatisfied need, or perhaps a feeling of sadness, fear, grief, embarrassment, or loneliness, the first feeling the person responds to is anger, because the tension beneath the anger is difficult to ignore.

A good exercise to use with your class is the Six Oranges conflict. The facilitator has six oranges, and two people in the class are fighting over which of them will get all six oranges. Both of them want all six and are unwilling to budge from their position. The conflict escalates to the point of name-calling and possible violence, when the facilitator asks class participants to see if they can come up with some possible compromise solutions that will satisfy both people.

When we use this example in classrooms, the students themselves quickly become frustrated and angry when the two people refuse to accept any of their solutions. Some solutions are quickly offered: "Give the oranges to the one who has the most money," "Grow more oranges," "Go to the store and buy more oranges," "If they won't share, don't give either one the oranges, keep them yourself. They're selfish." Other responses begin to be heard. "Cut the oranges in half and give each person six halves. That way they'll both get what they want—part of six oranges." "Let the one who needs the oranges for the most worthy purpose have them." Most students at some point get defensive or offensive, resorting to all the roadblocks to conflict resolution. Usually a student will ask the two, "Well, what do you want the oranges for anyway?" One says they have the flu and the doctor told them they need the juice of six oranges to get well. The other says they've promised to make a favorite orange cake for an aunt's birthday and need the rinds to bake the cake. All of a sudden, a genuine resolution to the problem is obvious—give the rinds to one, the juice to the other. Each student's solution to the problem was not the only one once the real problem was identified. People get into angry, attacking, defensive behaviors trying to force their personally preferred solution to a problem before the problem is accurately defined. Often the mere understanding of someone else's feelings and needs is enough to resolve a problem. The clear expression of feelings and needs is crucial to resolving conflicts if they are not to turn destructive through physical or emotional violence.

Reflective Listening

The goal of reflective listening is to assist the people in externalizing internal feelings and held-in problems and to help define them clearly so they can be understood by those involved in a conflict. It helps bridge the gap between a nonverbal mode of emotional intelligence and the verbal mode of cognitive intelligence, and allows the listener to serve as a mirror by continuing to reflect back to the speaker what the listener perceives and understands the speaker to mean in terms of thoughts and feelings. When this skill is used without any distorting roadblocks to another's authentic experience, it is a powerful means of helping the speaker identify what's going on inside—conflicts, feelings, thoughts—so they can actually hear it themselves, define the problem clearly, and find ways to resolve it either alone or in relationship to and with the support of others.

Refusing to control student behavior does not mean a teacher remains silent when one student is interfering with another's efforts to get needs met or deal with painful feelings. But in place of using roadblocks to control behavior, teachers can demonstrate (and model) self-control, self-expression, and self-disclosure. This is best done by delivering accurate, nonblaming "I-messages" that show the other person what needs are being interfered with and what the speaker is feeling. This is a way of respecting one's own needs and setting boundaries, while at the same time respecting the students' rights to get their needs met. This is a process that takes more time than merely—or momentarily—passing the problem over to another authority figure, but its long-range constructive effects on a teacher's relationship with a particular student and on the overall classroom environment are monumental. The teacher demonstrates self-discipline, self-control, competence, and mutual respect, instead of the common no-win control by punishment and reward.

A necessary piece to being an effective demonstrator, when beginning to set limits by self-disclosure instead of by fiat, is that of shifting gears when an I-message is met with defensiveness and resistance. Shifting gears means that the teacher has the patience and self-control to suspend, for the moment, getting a particular point across and instead being able to listen reflectively to the other person's resistance effectively enough for the other to say, "Yes, that's exactly how I feel about it." Once a listener has shown genuine empathy for the other person's point of view, the listener will in turn be ready to hear the teacher's original concern. Having done so, the teacher has a much greater chance of influencing the student's willingness to respect their point of view and needs without resorting to the usual devices of power and control.

Roadblocks to Communication

Thomas Gordon says, "We find that most parents and teachers are totally unaware of how often their everyday communication with children conveys nonacceptance and an intent to change them. Even adults who think that they are accepting and affirming are surprised to find out how frequently they communicate judgment and criticism" (176). After years of gathering responses in his classes, Gordon categorized the kinds of unhelpful responses—what he calls *roadblocks*. These include moralizing and preaching; advising, giving solutions; lecturing, teaching, and giving facts; judging, blaming, and criticizing; praising, buttering up; name-calling and ridiculing; interpreting, analyzing; reassuring and sympathizing; probing, questioning, and interrogating; withdrawing, diverting, or distracting. These kinds of responses are used all the time. What can replace these inadequate and often inappropriate attempts are the skills discussed above. It takes patience and practice to learn to listen instead of using roadblocks. The first step is recognizing the need for a different, more connected type of interaction.

Effective and attentive counselors learn these skills to use one-on-one with patients. Becoming adept as a good counselor is not the point here. But we have found that using these skills and demonstrating and modeling them with our students has been helpful. Students are encouraged to look at their own behavior and what influence it is having on others. This type of work has also been helpful in creating greater peace for each of us. Leaving the roles that Satir discusses behind, we encourage each of you to reflect on the kinds of behavior you expect from your students and yourself. We hope you will look further into the work of Gordon and Glasser and Satir for a changed perspective. As Carl Rogers said, "Prizing, loving feelings are not basically dangerous to give or receive, but are instead growth-promoting" (1969, 235). This is indeed emotional competence.

Works Cited

Glasser, W. 1998. *Choice Theory: A New Psychology of Personal Freedom.* New York: Harper Collins.

Goleman, D. 1995. *Emotional Intelligence.* New York: Bantam Books.

Gordon, T. 1989. *Discipline That Works: Promoting Self-Discipline in Children.* New York: Plume.

Roger, C. 1969. *Freedom to Learn (A View of What Education Might Become).* Columbus, OH: Merrill.

Satir, V., J. Stachowiak, and H. Taschman. 1975. *Helping Families to Change.* New York: Jason Aronson.

Using My Heart

Sally Gregory

Sally, who is a nationally certified counselor, currently teaches history in the Long Beach Unified School District and is an aquatics coach.

I teach tenth-grade Modern World History at a suburban high school in Los Angeles county with an average of thirty-six students in each of my periods. I teach students who are labeled "basic" by the system and have special education students identified as RSP and deaf/hard of hearing integrated into one of these classes. The numbers of students sometimes seem great to me because I am interested in learning about each and every one of them. I actually feel inadequate at times in my ability to be emotionally present with them. Yet I am learning how forgiving and generous my students can be of my inadequacies.

I posed three questions to my students:

1. How could I improve my learning and value my education?
2. How have any teachers helped my learning?
3. How does the classroom environment and teachers encourage individual responsibility and mutual respect?

Improve Our Education

Answers to the first question generally showed that the majority of students sought to please me. And in spite of my reassurance to them to be perfectly frank and honest, I am certain that they have learned the game of "flattery equals acceptance and approval by others." This disturbs me at times because I so want them to be free to question and learn the process and art of discussion.

There were one too many students who would write that the way to improve their education was to "try harder," "focus more," or "listen better." These responses sounded all too familiar. As family counselor JoAnne Ishimine (see this chapter) would diagnose, these were Placater responses, and not necessarily a heartfelt insight that connected them with what might need to change in their way of learning or within the learning environment. I do know that these students were attempting to be sincere and dutiful in their responses.

> Jeff Kerby (tenth grade): "I can improve my education and learning in many ways. The first way would be my self-motivation to learn. I can only learn if I have the desire to. If I don't think the subject is important, I won't have the desire to learn about it."

Caleb Engel (tenth grade): "I think I could improve my learning and education if we had more say in the types of classes we could take. I personally have a very hard time trying to learn when I have no interest whatsoever in the class. If I had a real choice in what classes I could take, I would probably do a whole lot better and learn a lot more. I also think the classes need to be smaller and more personal. School is being used the wrong way. Basically, it's one big holding tank for youth. The school's only goal is to have the kids stay within the parameters, not cause any trouble, and then graduate them. 'Our job is done, we educated them and kept them out of trouble, so no one can point the finger at them.' Learning isn't school's first goal."

Teachers Help Us

Students discussed our classroom processes in the second question, citing how valid group work and collaboration is for most of them. I know that groups can be a process of strain and discomfort for many students. The socialization and communication skills are uneven at this point for many teenagers, and the tendency for those who are uncomfortable is to withdraw or assume a low profile. I honor this for those students, because I believe greatly in the benefit of vicarious learning. Nevertheless, peer democratic influence can be a powerful guidance system for students. I continue to learn that the key is not to interfere with their problem solving and negotiations. I think it is all too tempting to want to autocratically set rigid guidelines for group interaction so as to gain a sense of some control and power with the level of energy going on and not allow for the process of partnerships and cohesion to genuinely take place. It is remarkable to see student reactions to the suggestion of forming new groups. Generally, this is not met with unconditional acceptance. Teenagers, if given the opportunity, demonstrate the power of group partnerships and cohesion. I usually allow them to stay with one another as long as they choose, and also to allow for some to negotiate a change to another group if they can work it out among themselves. This seems to result in students who feel empowered and honored for their ability to make their own judgments.

Encourage Individual Responsibility

The third question has been a source of discussion on our campus for some time. Mutual respect, honesty, and individual responsibility is more commonly seen among teenagers like those I learn with when they are acknowledged and validated for what I call their "adult abilities." One of the most difficult areas of power and control to loosen up on is that of assuming authority and wanting the students to validate them as teachers for it. It feels condescending to teenagers when adults talk at them as though the teens have no clue about life. If we would step back and really listen, observe, and absorb what young people have on their minds and hearts, we'd be amazed at the truly remarkable insights they have. It is hard for them to focus or to listen carefully when there is no invested relationship, interest, or motivation. It is easy to impose a double standard on students by expecting them to do things that we often find difficult to demand of ourselves. I encourage students to consider their motives for the day, to examine what they need to do to take care of their own business so they might be in a better place for listening to a slide lecture or working in their groups. I have no problem with students eating in my class, writing notes, and reading if they assume responsibility for the outcome of perhaps being preoccupied that day, realizing that they may have affected how efficiently a group was able to work, or might miss something that was discussed. Of course, we agree that they will be as courteous with the classroom environment as they are with each other. We agree that each student will take responsibility for anything that they may miss but need to take individual responsibility to work it out with me or their groups.

> Beth Moody (tenth grade): "Ms. G's class environment is laid back. Sometimes other teachers' respect are like in your face with their attitudes. She shows us respect and shows respect to other staff. She doesn't razz any of us for not knowing an answer, instead she helps to understand it. But at the same time she gently pushes us to try to seek understanding. That's just how she is."

JoAnne Ishimine is correct. School ignores too much of the child. We are wrapped up in "performance-based acceptance," responding to cognitive needs but not emotional ones. As my students clearly state, supported by the survey responses from the entire school, students have unmet needs. There is always an element of performing in life— playing a role. But as educators we tend to take the "life" part out of performing. Imagine providing an environment where each student can experience success in knowing themselves and how to get along with others. As Jake says, "Do what you love and love what you do." That skill requires much from the educational community. The next essay describes an important set of tasks that our school has undertaken to explore the issues of respect and care.

What Teachers Need to Do to Change: Summary of Student Survey

Students from the Long Beach Unified School District

Origins of the Student Survey

In 1994, Marvin Holmes decided to stop being a corporate business-man and begin working in a field where he felt he could have a greater impact. Hired at Lakewood High School in Southern California, he teaches in the Business-Technology department. During his first year of teaching he heard students complain about the lack of respect they received from teachers. Of course, he was accustomed to hearing from teachers how respect needed to be "earned" by the students. Concerned, he gathered together a few interested teachers to encourage an open discussion about how teachers could be more aware of the need for mutual respect between teachers and their students. Many inspirational flyers and meetings later the school-based Site Council voted to formally add the Mutual Respect Committee, chaired by Mr. Holmes. The MRC is comprised of six teachers, three students, and one parent.

The questions on the survey that follows were generated by Mr. Holmes and his students. One hundred and twenty ninth- through twelfth-grade typing students were given the surveys and eighty-one were returned. The survey discloses the important insights the students had about teachers' behavior toward them. After showing the MRC and administrators the results, there was overwhelming approval to share the results of the survey to the faculty for their input.

The committee decided to role-play two actual scenarios that had happened on campus between students and teachers during a staff development day. Afterward, facilitators broke the teachers into small groups and shared what could have been alternative responses for the scenarios. Most teachers were sincere in their attempts to share and own some of what they may do themselves. Yet Mr. Holmes received some very vocal negative feedback from teachers who thought his efforts were offensive to their sense of professionalism. Interestingly, it was these teachers who chose not to get involved in actively cultivating mutual respect.

Every teacher received the results of the survey and the comments the teachers shared during the staff development. Following this, one teacher who was offended by the process came to a Site Council meeting and insisted that a second survey be made that emphasized that the responsibility for mutual respect be placed squarely on the shoulders of the students. Such a survey was constructed and was recently given to teachers for their voluntary input. I am certain that many teachers will cooperate and the teachers and students will receive the results of the survey.

Mr. Holmes and the Mutual Respect Committee have indeed caught the attention of teachers on campus, but more important, have taken risks that have resulted in significant steps to give students an opportunity to become empowered and to give them a real chance to be heard.

Student Responses to the Survey

1. The best kind of teachers are the ones who care. If the teacher doesn't care, then the students will sense it and then they won't care. Show respect. Establish a friendly relationship with students. Be our role models. Encourage. Be optimistic.

2. Listen to what I have to say. Listen to students' requests and complaints.

3. Treat students with respect. Put yourselves in the student's place and see if that's how you would like to be treated. Try to understand the student's point of view. Have patience and understand that we're going through our teen years and we sometimes get crazy. Remember you went through it too.

4. Make class interesting for the students. If the class is boring the students are going to be bored and not want to go to class. It's hard to learn when it's hard to stay awake (don't be boring).

5. Students would get more involved in class if it was fun! Make learning fun, not always serious. If the teacher is fun and everyone gets along with them there is a greater chance that the students will focus more and want to learn and won't want to let the teacher down. Make the class fun and it wouldn't be so bad, we might enjoy the class.

6. Actually teach what you want us to learn, not just tell us to do something that we don't know how to do. A lot of teachers just give us work and we're supposed to figure it out on our own. Listen to all questions that students have.

7. Calm down when things don't go your way. Be patient. Sometimes teachers tend to come to class already in a bad mood. They should leave it out of the class. Lighten up, all people make mistakes.

8. Some teachers don't care if their students graduate or not. Some teachers don't interact with their students. Get more involved. Be friendly to your students.

9. Don't talk down to your students. Don't make us feel like crap. Control your tempers, you are supposed to be the adults. Never disrespect students in front of the class, they are just setting themselves up for that student to rebel against them in front of the class. Teachers can lower our self-esteem.

7

Self-Evaluation as a Tool for Quality

Our Invitation

Chapter 7 is about self-evaluation. A powerful message that schools send to children is that their work must be judged by an outside adult authority. Children hear, "Do it my way and then I'll tell you if you have done it well." In life, however, we need to self-evaluate in order to be successful. How can we create classrooms where children learn to evaluate their own work and behavior in order to do their best? Students from Sharon Setoguchi's class describe how important this process has been for their learning and Sharon shares the rationale and process she has developed. This chapter discusses specific strategies and practices to move your classroom toward responsible student-led self-evaluation.

Self-Evaluation: Grading So It Really Matters

J. Cynthia McDermott

J. Cynthia McDermott teaches teachers at California State University–Dominguez Hills in Los Angeles.

I once heard psychiatrist William Glasser say that statistician W. Edwards Deming believed that no human should *ever* evaluate another human being. What a shocking statement! As I thought about it I began to understand something I'd learned, but didn't know I'd learned, when I was in school. When teachers grade, that is judge and evaluate their students, children come to learn that they must look to others to figure out how they are doing. Teachers grade papers, correct grammar, check answers, tell students how long the paper should be and then determine if the student has reached the mark. Years of external evaluation make children dependent on the "authority" to "know" how they're doing. This is the way it has been done in schools for a very long time, but as this chapter explores, perhaps there is another way.

Look more closely at what kind of thinker external evaluation creates. When teachers grade papers and tests, with the hope of seeing their students perform well, it is because they want their students to excel—to do their best. If a student receives a B, it is because it is not as good as an A, and the teacher hopes that next time the student will try to do A work. Unfortunately, this process never takes into account whether the student genuinely understands what A work looks like, or if they even feel any need to receive an A. If Glasser and others are right and students choose their behavior to get their needs met, then doing well and feeling competent in school may or may not be important. Punishing a student with a lowered grade will not increase their motivation to do A work. In fact, it will probably accomplish quite the opposite result (see Alfie Kohn's chapter for further discussion). But let's return to Deming.

W. Edwards Deming was a statistician who was hired by General MacArthur to help the Japanese improve the quality of production in factories after the Second World War. His success is well documented in the quality movement literature. We can see how successful merely by looking at how quickly the world came to measure quality by Japanese standards, including electronics and automobiles. So what did Deming do? He convinced manufacturers to end the practice of external evaluation.

A brief story about the McDermott Widget Corporation might serve as an example. You work at WidgCorp making widgets. In order to be paid, you must meet company production quotas and manufacture twenty-three widgets to company specifications. These guidelines were developed by someone above you; they are the rules by which you work. The floor manager must make sure that each of the workers makes their twenty-three widgets. Each day your widgets are checked to company standards. Each day your production output is evaluated. If management is satisfied, you get paid. Everyone works to the expectations; no one makes twenty-four widgets a day. Everyone is happy, right? Perhaps. Now along comes a new lead manager who challenges the other managers by saying, "Your new job is to help develop strategies for making not more, but better widgets. Work with your employees to produce as many quality widgets as they can. Oh, and by the way, have your employees self-evaluate their work."

What kind of widget will be produced in this kind of environment? As the Japanese discovered, with Deming's help, creating environments that encouraged individuals to do their best work, by their own standards of self-evaluation, produced quality products and workers who were more intrinsically satisfied with their jobs. Quality became an internal, self-realized marker.

Do you know when you've "manufactured" a great lesson and one that hasn't proved successful? Do you know when you've spoken eloquently or written well? You usually do. But for many, having been taught not only to be judgmental, but to rely on the judgments (and grades) of others, we lose sight of our own internal markers—and the ability to assess and reflect on our efforts. This deeply ingrained process is very difficult to change for most of us, and for most of our students as well.

Perhaps seeing student work improve and hearing children express satisfaction with their efforts will be what will convince you to try a Deminglike approach. What would it be like, for example, if you could self-critique what went well and what didn't when your principal visits your class to grade *you?* Using self-evaluation, students at all levels can learn to do critical analyses of their own academic and affective work.

I would like to explain the self-evaluation process that I use with the students I teach. The primary reason I came to dislike grading students is because of the obvious disparity in student understanding any class has at the beginning of a term, one student to the next. This was compounded by my lack of success in determining what students knew by the end of the term. When I teach a methods course, I try to model teaching practices rather than talk about them, and one semester I decided to model Deming's approach of worker self-evaluation and job satisfaction. I asked my students to keep a portfolio of all their work and then at the end of the semester to create a performance portfolio to use in a demonstration of their learning.

Also, I told my students they were expected to negotiate with me for their course grade. Several powerful things happened. Some students were delighted to share their "products" but had a difficult time talking about what they had learned. Others were very nervous about negotiating their grade and refused in the end to do so. On the other hand, a number of students were delighted with the process and shared with me important steps that had challenged their thinking in my class as well as the practices they had tried with their students. The main difficulties of this presentation process were the time-intensive work for me (I often have forty students in a class) and the difficulty many students had in asking for their grade.

After reflecting on this first semester's experiment, I made some changes. At the end of the second semester, I met with students in pairs, which helped the time constraint and some of the students' awkwardness. I felt, however, that most students were taking the opportunity to tell me what they liked about the class, rather than reflecting on what they had learned. I needed to increase our time with, and deepen our efforts toward, reflection. It is, for me, *the* underused and undervalued educational tool.

With the third semester, I began using "reflection cards" each class session, an idea I learned from Cliff Knapp. The students and I talked about reflection in class and used the last fifteen minutes for students to write, on five-by-eight-inch cards, about anything. Each week I responded to their comments, which ranged from "Nothing tonight," to two cards full of personal thoughts and questions about class. As students began to practice the habit of weekly reflection, I noticed many start to keep journals and begin to incorporate reflection with their own students. I began to more systematically ask questions on their cards so they could get at what was changing for them in their thinking as a result of the course. That semester the class decided to try an informal reflective self-evaluation based on questions I designed to serve as criteria for the process. The students, I'm glad to say, were patient with my experimentation. I constructed a number of broad questions about our work together, and the students wrote responses and gave themselves a grade at the conclusion of their reflection. It went well and the students felt the process was enlightening, although very difficult.

After several semesters, the self-evaluation process is still growing and changing—and reflects the personality and efforts of the students of any given class. It continues to be designed by me with student input. I introduce the concept of a self-evaluation process at the beginning of the course. After that, the students and I create the course syllabus together during the first two nights of class. We then decide on the self-evaluation process. This early determination of expectations seems helpful to the students.

In my classes there are "Givens," which are my nonnegotiable requirements, and of course there are the departmental requirements.

Also, students are invited to contribute their own Givens to the ones I present. The Givens are both content- and process-specific. I take responsibility to prepare the final evaluation guidelines, composed mainly of questions aimed toward reflection, soon after the syllabus is finished to guide ongoing discussion and decision making. The questions change depending on the course, but a current version of the Givens and final evaluation guidelines for a course called Interdisciplinary Methods are presented here in the form given to the students.

Course Givens TED 469

1. Explore and develop an understanding of the interdisciplinary process beyond the traditional notion of "content" as discipline.

2. Explore varying views of the constructivist classroom, particularly student-centered approaches, through theory, practice, and research.

3. Define self-evaluation and determine how to do it, including learning reflection skills.

4. Read assigned text and other materials.

5. Work together as a class and create a deliberate community, resolving all conflicts.

6. Do a quality job. Be a memorable student.

7. Design and complete a project with the class that demonstrates the use of interdisciplinary skills.

Final Evaluation TED 469

Self-evaluation gives you the opportunity to reflect on your work in this class, to determine the quality of your work, and to convince me that your decision about your grade is appropriate. I usually suggest that students write a response in a letter format as it seems to create an informality that is useful. You may, however, decide to write answers to each of these concerns. Risk is an important part of learning, and I am particularly interested in those areas where you may have decided to allow yourself some discomfort and entertain ideas or perspectives you may not have heard before. And above all, be honest with yourself. You will be happier with the result. Thanks for your thoughtfulness. Most student responses are at least three pages if typed. Your final evaluation does not need to be typed, but if your penmanship is difficult to read, please type. Also, some students have chosen other methods for response, such as videos, audiotapes, and presentations.

Review the Givens of the course. Comment on how much you have achieved in understanding them. How much effort did you commit? If you were not clear about an idea, what did you do to change that? What processes did you think about using that you were reluctant to use? Why did you hesitate, if you did?

Given #1. Are you clear about the various models you read and saw? Could you define them? Could you conduct an inservice using the information you have? Do you have an opinion about the usefulness and opportunity of interdisciplinary work? Can you now articulate what this new field is about and how it might fit into the existing curriculum?

Given #2. What is your understanding of constructivism? Whose work fuels this point of view? Why do they believe what they believe? What happens to students (you) when this kind of model is presented? Using yourself for research, did you try to take advantage of this powerful new model? Were you willing to look at your own point of view and articulate it to me? Were you engaged in helpful dialogue to create support and forward movement to practice this model? Are you able to engage in this type of teaching now? What, for you, is the significance of experiencing the model instead of reading about it?

Given #3. Did you keep up with the reflections? Did you write each week? Did you engage in reflective practices using the cards? Did you incorporate reflection in your own classes? Did you teach your students to become reflective? Did you stand back and reflect on your own teaching to determine what could be done to improve your work? Did you act on your reflections? When and how?

Given #4. Did you read all the material I gave you? Did you think about the ideas presented or forget what you read by the time you got to the bottom of the page? What new ideas did the authors offer? Did the readings reinforce beliefs you already held, or challenge you to rethink some of your assumptions? What was your opinion of the readings? Will they influence your teaching? Did you take time to explore the library or professional journals or any of the texts I introduced to expand your preservice perspective?

Given #5. Did you work with the class to create a more caring community? Were you a positive participant? Were you a memorable student? When things concerned you or upset you, did you try to change them in a positive fashion? Did you attend class in order to contribute your ideas and thoughts to the entire group? Were you reliable and dependable? Were you an active participant and listener during class discussions? Did the "talk" create new ideas for you? If you were bored, what else could you have done? If you were confused, what might you have done differently? Did you put in the anticipated time? Why or why not? Did you have any conflicts during our course? Did you add to the process of resolution? Did you carry this skill into your classroom with your students or master teacher? If there was a conflict, are you proud of the way you handled it? Was your behavior professional?

Given #6. Quality work means doing your very best. Not the best according to others, but what you feel is YOUR best, with no excuses. You had a great deal of freedom in this class, and it is tempting for students to do only what is necessary in order to pass. Only you know what you are capable of. Did you do your best? Did the work you do reflect a quality effort? If your students performed at the level you did in this course, would you think it was quality work?

Given #7. Did you do a project? Is it completed? Are you proud of it? Did you put your best thinking into it? What did you learn from doing it? Why did you do it? Will it prove helpful to you? Did you take my challenge and create an opportunity for the development of something that will enhance the experiences of your students?

Overall performance. So, how did you do? Are you pleased with your effort? Did you do your best? Did you fall short in any area that you might improve if you took the course again? Finally, what else of importance would you like to share with me?

Grading. Please evaluate yourself on each Given on a scale from one to five, five representing the most memorable student you have ever known, and one representing one who delivers a barely acceptable effort. There are a possible 35 points available for the course. Using a traditional scale, 35 = 100% (A); 32 = 90% (B+); 30 = 85% (B); 28 = 80% (B–); 23 = 75% (C). What grade do you feel you earned for this course knowing your potential and ability? Once I read your letter and understand your rationale for the grade you feel you earned, I will either enter your requested grade, or in those cases where I feel you have underrated or overrated your efforts, will raise or drop the grade.

One of my students said it well. "I think about what grade I should receive here, and it is obvious to me that most people who take a college class should take the class wanting an A. But what good is that mark anyway? What constitutes an A, and who is to say? This whole thing about grades is starting to wear on me. I have another class, and the teacher is so concerned with the points, the grade, the percentage, that it takes away from what the class is about. I found myself totaling up my points during class time to see where I stood. DURING CLASS TIME, INSTEAD OF LISTENING! It drove me nuts when I realized what I was doing. So I really have thought about what I do to my students as well. This process of evaluating myself has been so liberating. I focused on what I was learning and not what I was expected to produce. Thanks for the opportunity." Remarks like Steve's have become increasingly common as students participate in a process that in theory, perhaps, once sounded silly or absurd.

A significant change occurred last semester. Points and percentages are gone because they feel too much like the traditional measure of evaluation where the numbers control the decision. (They are still helpful for some students who have a hard time figuring out where they are on the continuum, so I have presented that model here.) As I have become more comfortable with this process, I can reassure most students that they really do know how they have done and that they can trust me to trust them in their self-assessments. Establishing that trust is critical and something we work on the entire semester. If my goal is to help students decide what they do well and encourage them to do their best, then I feel strongly that they should control the entire evaluation process.

There are several weaknesses remaining. First, I have not weighted the categories, although in my mind they have variable values. The class and I discuss this, and I have opted to leave them unweighted. A second weakness is that some students, even at the preservice level, underestimate themselves or value their work less highly than I (or others) do. I call students to discuss this after I receive their evaluations, but many students stand firm. "I didn't do my best." Many of my students have been "good" students throughout their educational careers, receiving high marks fairly easily. These students can be particularly hard on themselves, judging themselves too harshly. I remind them of Deming's regard for external judging of others, and the impact it can have on lifelong learners.

A third concern is that students can take advantage of the self-evaluation process. I suppose it can happen, but the entire focus of the course is on responsibility and trust and taking risks. So telling lies runs counter to the moral code of the class. Now if I didn't teach Glasser's Choice Theory and Deming's model for self-evaluation and why it is helpful, then I would expect abuse. But my students are moving toward understanding by participating in a process that they have never tried before. The level of honesty continues to be very high. Of course, there are always exceptions, and the exception clause in the grading section is for those students to clearly understand the difference between self-evaluation and a free grade.

Average grades for my courses run no higher than those of my colleagues, and are often lower. I have had students give themselves an F, and I comply with student "requests" for Ds and Cs. Interestingly, these students are still able to clearly articulate what they have learned, and do so.

But what makes this grading process work? Why bother trying this? What might be helpful in a classroom of younger students?

In the 1970s, Dr. William Glasser, a certified psychiatrist by trade, wrote *Schools Without Failure* as a challenge to the way our schools have traditionally operated and graded students. In it, he began to present a concise view of behavior and its effects. Opposing the popular stimulus-response model, Glasser believes that we choose our behaviors in order to fulfill needs. Once called Control Theory, he now calls this model Choice Theory. Glasser believes that we are genetically programmed to choose our behaviors in order to get four basic psychological needs met: love and belonging, power (being listened to), fun (inner satisfaction), and freedom. We choose our behaviors to satisfy one or more of these needs. Although quite a sophisticated theory, it is elegantly simple as well.

Most of us (including teachers) believe that we can make someone do what we want, particularly if we have more power (money, position, strength, authority). We have been taught such, directly and indirectly, since childhood. We believe that we can offer rewards to get good behavior and punishments to change bad behavior. But that belief best describes how we train dogs. We offer them incentives and we either reward or punish them, depending on how well they obey our commands. Most of the research done for this external motivation model used dogs and birds. I wonder why cats were never used? Cats are rarely interested in our pleas or ministrations. They eat when they want, go where they want, do what they want. The typical rewards and punishments for dogs do not work for most cats. Children are far more sophisticated than cats and yet we expect them to behave like dogs. Perhaps our thinking needs to change.

Choice Theory is a model that recognizes that we are in control of our behavior. Sometimes we as teachers, as well as our students, choose inappropriate or incorrect behavior; sometimes certain behavior is anti-social. But Glasser discovered that by using Choice Theory and a method of helping others make decisions he called Reality Therapy, people could learn to make new choices and replace unhelpful or unhealthy ones. Skills could be learned and practiced (see JoAnne Ishimine's chapter).

Imagine a classroom where students begin to understand that they choose how they behave and willingly learn to make new choices to become a memorable student. What could you do to help your students? Teaching them the basic elements of Choice Theory is necessary. When students, in a learning environment, realize they can manage their own behavior, their efforts and involvements change. Ask them to reflect on something they are working on. Ask them how their work is coming along. Is it turning out the way they expected? (See Cliff Knapp's chapter for more ideas.) Help them choose what to do next. Once they have completed a project, ask them to evaluate if it is the best work they are capable of—Glasser would ask if it is a quality job. What would it take—time, materials, assistance—to make it better?

Asking children to evaluate a product of theirs and perhaps even to give it a grade is a first step. But what you are really after is for kids to evaluate their *learning,* and themselves as learners, as active community members, as people. It is easy to stay at the product evaluation level; we get stuck there all the time. But ask students what kind of learner they think they are, what kind of member of the classroom community. Is what they are learning helping them in other parts of their lives? And as you get more comfortable you can ask them for feedback about the class, and perhaps about your teaching efforts. The most advanced stage would be for students to create their own project and then evaluate and grade their individual progress and growth, as well as the product, and reflect on implications for their futures.

To some adults, this process of self-evaluation remains an unacceptable practice. After all, grading is the job of the teacher. I have found that nothing will convince such people better than simply listening to children talk about how self-evaluation and reflection have changed the quality of their learning experiences. A helpful procedure for showing (rather than just explaining) this to parents and administrators is the student-led conference, a recent addition to the evaluation process designed to help students present to their parents (and teachers) what they've learned and to reflect on that learning effort. To get started, students must begin collecting work for a portfolio. If students have been taught Choice Theory, reflection, and active listening skills, they will be more prepared to move in this direction. In preparation for the conference, parents are invited to meet at the school with, and only with, the student. Parents are asked to listen for the first twenty minutes and then are invited to ask questions during the last ten minutes.

The student needs to create a presentation plan that can be done as a class. For example, the class could list some of the things they have done and create the guidelines to describe self-evaluation. Then students show their parents their portfolio. This process is extraordinarily powerful because the child is demonstrating as well as explaining what they have learned. (To save time, four conferences can occur simultaneously with the teacher nearby. This usually increases conference participation time significantly.) When parents leave, they are asked to write a letter to their child, in which they are invited to reflect on the conference. The student-led conference is a marvelous way to involve parents as well as students in the learning process.

Self-evaluation is a powerful process by which teachers and students choose to become active learners as well as assume greater responsibility for their behaviors. As you begin to think about self-evaluation, try using the process with your teaching. How did it go? What one thing could I have done to help a particular student be more successful? As you become comfortable, read and use Glasser's ideas. Think about helping children understand that they can choose "good" behaviors. Help them begin to assess their own work. Instead of saying, "What a great story," or "What a wonderful drawing," or just plain "Terrific!" ask the students to "judge" their own work. As you coach your children to be self-evaluators, you are teaching them a lifelong skill toward becoming critical thinkers.

Students Can Grade Themselves

Sharon Setoguchi

Grades have always frustrated me, both as a student and as a teacher. So one of the first things I discuss with my students each year is the concept of grades and grading. I begin by asking, "How many of you have ever received a grade lower than you expected or than you felt you deserved?" Not surprisingly, almost every hand goes up. Then I ask, "How many of you have ever received a grade higher than you deserved?" Again, almost every hand is raised. Most of the time, students know whether or not they have done good work, how much effort they have put into a class, and whether they have learned anything in a class. Given the opportunity, they will be critically candid about the grades they have received.

When I first began teaching, the idea of having my students grade themselves never even occurred to me. Yet as hard as I tried, I found it impossible to remain completely objective when determining grades. The more I tried to create an unemotional, objective policy, the more subjective and unfair the process seemed to be. And, inevitably, after every grade report was issued, some student would come to me questioning why they had received the grade they did. Students would argue over every point, afraid that one point would be the dividing line between an A or a B. Although most of the time it was not, sometimes the difference between 89.4 percent (a B) and 89.5 percent (an A) was *exactly* one point. Much of the time, I felt as if I were a "grade police officer" rather than a teacher.

After that first year, I decided to try having students evaluate themselves. Not willing to risk having students determine their final grades out of fear that they would give themselves the grade they wanted instead of the grade they had earned, I began by asking students to grade themselves on individual assignments. We would determine a rubric or grading scale for a particular assignment as a class, then students would grade themselves according to that criteria. However, I was still in control of the grades since I controlled the discussion about the grading scale. Students were unwilling or unable to take a hard look at what they had done. To my disappointment, grades were a few points higher than they would have been had I assigned the grade.

At that point, I experimented with having students set goals for themselves before we began a project or extended writing piece. I asked students to decide individually what they wanted to learn or accomplish and how they wanted to be evaluated *before* they began their work. At the end of the project, I had students grade themselves based on the goals they had set before the project began.

Through this effort, I realized the value of self-evaluation. Students were actually talking to me about what they had learned! They were beginning to be critics of their own work and looked for ways to improve upon what they had begun. They would tell where they had worked hard and where they had "slacked off." My students would say things like "I didn't spend enough time researching my topic," or "This could have been better if I had done a second interview." They could evaluate their own strengths and weaknesses. More important, they had begun to set their own criteria and then assess whether or not they had done a quality job. What surprised me the most was that students were now giving themselves lower grades than I expected, rather than higher.

The following year, I began to have students set semester goals and then evaluate themselves at the end of the semester. I had learned that two of the most important factors in self-evaluation were goal setting and the discussion of quality. If I wanted my students to set high standards for themselves, I had to help them understand the concept of doing quality work (as McDermott describes in her discussion of Deming's work).

How did I help students understand what "quality work" is? I decided to ask about something that is important in most of my students' lives. I asked them where they would shop if they were looking for "A"-quality shoes. Students agreed that Foot Locker was the place to shop for good shoes. Then I asked where they would find shoes that were "C" quality. Answers varied, but students got the idea. From then on, we were able to look at work as being "Foot Locker–quality" or something less than that. It wasn't long before I could ask my students if they had done a "quality job" on an assignment to get them to critically reflect on the work they had done.

At the end of the year, I asked students to define quality as part of their final evaluation. One student phrased it better than I could have myself: "Quality is trying your hardest to do the very best job you can do and being proud to sign your name to the finished product."

That same year, I had one student who consistently graded himself higher than I felt was justified. On his ten-week and fifteen-week self-evaluation, he would honestly assess what he had done well and what he could have done better. He also acknowledged where he had fallen short of his own goals and of my expectations. To my dismay, he still ended up giving himself an A. Try as I might during individual conferences with this student, I could not seem to get him to understand that an A did not coincide with his overall self-evaluation.

After much self-reflection of my own, I decided to trust in the process I had committed to and let the A stand. While I know that many of my colleagues would feel that this was unfair to other students or was a kind of "grade inflation," I realized that if I was going to ask students to grade themselves, I had to trust their judgment and they had to believe that I trusted them. I hoped that by respecting this young man's self-evaluation, he would be motivated to improve the quality of his work and do the kind of work which we both would agree was A-quality work.

Unfortunately, at the twenty-week semester evaluation, this student again gave himself an A despite the fact that his written comments did not justify an A. I was truly disappointed. I asked him to stay after school to discuss his self-evaluation. While he agreed with my assessment that he had not met either his own goals or my stated goals for the semester, he insisted that he should receive the A. He seemed angry at me for suggesting that I might have to lower the grade. When I explained that I felt I had an obligation to maintain a certain standard of quality, he became stone-faced and silent. All the time I had spent trying to establish a positive rapport with this young man evaporated in a few minutes.

At that point, I gave in. I told him that while I was not comfortable with the grade and not happy with him or with myself, I would let the A stand. He turned and asked if that made me a quality teacher. Out of hurt and anger, I responded with scorching honesty, "No, but if I were a 'quality' teacher, you would not be giving yourself an A. But I believe that if this A is so important that you would lie to yourself and me, it must be very, very important. My only consolation is that I have been true to my word. I said I wouldn't change a grade without your consent and I won't."

As I spoke, tears began to roll down my student's face. Shocked, I asked more gently what the problem was. At last, he told me why the A was so important. He knew that he was expected to come home with all As and that the consequences for anything less would be severe. He told me that since he knew he could give himself an A in my class, doing work for my class was not as high a priority as for other classes. He said, "My parents will kill me if I come home with a B."

After a few minutes more of discussion, he told me he would give 110 percent the following semester if I would "let him have the A." I told him the decision was his to make and that I trusted that whatever decision he made, it would be the right one for him, his parents, and me. He decided that A would be his semester grade. I accepted his decision. Although I was still a little disappointed, I tried not to let it show. I also worried about setting a precedent that I would not be able to continue with, but decided to honor his decision anyway.

It wasn't until the next evaluation that I realized why my decision had been the right one. The young man wrote a three-page evaluation detailing what goals he had set, what he understood to be my expectations, and what he had accomplished and not accomplished. Then he wrote, "One goal I set for myself was to be completely honest with myself and with you. You trusted my decision last semester, and I will never forget what that felt like. I discussed this evaluation with my parents last night. We agreed that since I had not reached the goals I had set to my satisfaction, I should receive a B. I don't think I'll ever have the courage to tell my parents what happened last semester, but last night we had our first ever conversation about grades and about the pressure they put on me."

This young man taught me how important trust is in the process of self-evaluation. It is, without a doubt, the single most important factor in helping students become self-reflective. I have to trust that my students will be honest with themselves and with me. I have to take the time to discuss quality work and discuss my goals and expectations for them. If I want them to be honest with themselves, I must be honest with myself and with them. When I say that I will not change the grades they give themselves, they have to know that they can trust what I say. I want to help them see that when we reflect on our own learning, we are doing so in order to help ourselves learn more the next time. I try to help them understand that doing "Foot Locker–quality work" is for their own satisfaction and not mine.

When I achieve these goals, I am never disappointed with the grades that end up in my roll book. Students are as honest with me and with themselves as I am with them and with myself. Self-reflection and self-evaluation help all of us "try our hardest to do the very best job we can do and be proud to sign our names on the finished product."

Self-Evaluation Is Good for Students

Seventh-grade students at Stephen M. White Middle School, Los Angeles

The following conversation was held after the students in Sharon Setoguchi's class had completed their first semester self-evaluation. Ms. Setoguchi invited her students to have a conversation with her about self-evaluation. These students have been participating in this process for one or two years.

Many thanks to all the students in my 1997–98 Period 1 English class for their hard work, but special thanks to these students: Harvey Brimbuela, Krystal Toure, David Cordero, Ascot Tabucan, Edgar Morales, Mayra Moran, Cristina Herrera, Ruzelle Nocon, Richard Raquel, Zer Reyes, Claudia Luna, Abe Baquir, Laurie Virtusio, and Carlos Cortez.

Ms. S.: What do you think about self-evaluation? Is it a good thing, or would you rather we didn't use it in our class?

Harvey: Self-evaluation is good for students. It is good because the teachers just look at our work. Our work may not show how much effort we really put into it. Some students try really hard to do good work, but sometimes it just doesn't come out exactly right.

Carlos: Right. Some people learn a lot, but their work doesn't show it.

David: Personally, I think the idea of self-evaluation is very bothersome. I don't understand why we have to grade ourselves. Most teenagers are not very honest, and thus, get grades they do not deserve.

Ms. S.: That's a good point. What do others think about that? Is self-evaluation unfair?

Zer: I think most people are honest enough to give themselves an appropriate grade. Most students would have some guilt if they gave themselves a perfect grade and didn't earn it.

Richard: Exactly. When you give yourself a good grade that you don't deserve, you feel stupid.

Harvey: But some students take advantage of this system. These students know they are doing bad, but they still give themselves a good grade.

Ms. S.: Isn't it tempting to take advantage of the system?

Edgar: Of course. At first, everyone thinks they will give themselves an A. But once they get their chance, it's not that easy. You think, "What do I deserve?" You might think about giving yourself a wrong grade, but you know you deserve a bad grade. That makes things very difficult.

Claudia: On the other hand, I think sometimes I'm too hard on myself. It is way easier to just ask what your grade is in the class. When you grade yourself, you have to always try to do the most possible because you set the standard yourself.

Ms. S.: Oh, so grading yourself makes you work harder?

Claudia: Exactly. Self-evaluation is hard for me because I realize what I have and *haven't* done.

Abe: Yes. I know what I am capable of, and I am forced to give myself the grade I deserve. With other teachers, I don't have to try my hardest, but I can still get an A because of their grading scale.

Harvey: I think that's because we know how hard we really try, and we know what we can do. Students *are* harder on themselves than the teacher usually is.

Laurie: For me, knowing that you grade yourself in this class is relaxing. You don't have to please the teacher, but yourself. You *want* to push an extra mile to do whatever you can do. It gives students control of their grade, rather than giving it to the teacher who may not even know your name.

Ms. S.: I'd like to hear more about that. How does being asked to evaluate yourself affect your relationship with me, your teacher?

Mayra: Most teachers don't really care about what students think. The fact that you let us give ourselves a grade shows that you trust us to tell you how much we have really tried. It makes me glad that I actually have a teacher who actually cares about what I think and can trust me even after I might not deserve a lot because of how I was in the past. Most teachers won't give us second or third chances.

Harvey: Self-evaluation is all about being honest with the teacher and with yourself.

Mayra: Yeah, grading myself helps me to be more honest with myself. I see how much I have tried and how much more I need to improve.

Ms. S.: So when students are honest in their self-evaluations, does it affect the quality of their work?

Cristina: Yes, because you get to see how well you are doing and what you need to improve on. It makes you want to do your work. You see what grade you really deserve and want to do better the next time.

Krystal: Grading myself does, in fact, affect what work I do and how I do it. It gives me a chance to reflect and see where I am, what I've done, what I haven't done, and where I really slacked off.

Ascot: With self-evaluation, you have to think about whether you gave your full effort and participation in the classroom and your group. It's always helpful because it helps students concentrate on studying, not on the grade.

Ms. S.: What does that mean "concentrate on studying, not on the grade"?

Carlos: Since students decide on their own grade based on what they have learned, the student can study without worrying about getting a bad grade. When you get nervous, it's easy not to do well on a test even if you know a lot about the subject.

Ruzelle: You're worrying about doing well on the test, so you focus on the grade you want. You might remember the information for the test, but you haven't really learned anything because you weren't focused on learning.

Ms. S.: Is self-evaluation helpful in any other way?

Cristina: Yes. It makes you think about why other teachers give you the grades you get. It has actually helped me do better in other classes.

Mayra: I think it has helped me to actually think about how well educated I can be. Now I want to improve more and more in all my classes.

Ms. S: Then would you like the opportunity to evaluate yourself in all your classes?

Edgar: It would be OK to have this in all classes, but at some point you wish you didn't. It's easier to get a good grade from the teacher because you know what they expect and can work up to that level.

Ms. S.: As I have seen from your comments, even though not everyone sees the same worth in the process, self-evaluation has substantially changed the focus of our class from obsessing about grades to conversations about learning. That, in itself, makes self-evaluation valuable for all of us.

8

Social Responsibility and Learning for Life

Our Invitation

Chapter 8 is written by Shelley Berman, founder of Educators for Social Responsibility. He has updated his classic work, "The Real Ropes Course," to describe how social responsibility and meaningful schools help children become contributing members of a democratic society. Administrators and faculty from Wayland, Massachusetts, respond.

The Real Ropes Course:
The Development of Social Consciousness

Sheldon Berman

Sheldon is the superintendent of schools in Hudson, MA, and the past president of Educators for Social Responsibility.

We live in a complex time. There are few simple answers to the complicated issues we face. Children become aware of the trauma in the world around them at a far earlier age than we would like and often lack the skills to deal with its complexity. In our efforts to preserve their childhood, we often allow important issues to go undiscussed and attitudes of cynicism, hopelessness, and powerlessness to develop. This need not be the case. Social, political, and ethical reflection and action build empowerment by peeling back the layers that underlie our values. Helping young people find within themselves the strengths and commitments to make a difference for themselves, others, and the planet as a whole teaches that what we do matters. It matters to those who love us. It matters to those with whom we work and play. It matters to us and helps us experience integrity. And what we do matters to the world as it is now as well as to how it will be in the future. Each of our actions—and our failures to act—sets in motion a steady series of ripples through our environment and our lives.

Social responsibility—that is, a personal investment in the well-being of others and of the planet—doesn't just happen. It takes intention, attention, and time. It may even take redesigning the culture of schools and classrooms to one that esteems and creates empowerment, cooperation, compassion, and respect. This chapter is about ways to develop social responsibility.

What the Research Tells Us

Prosocial behavior and activism are stimulated by the unity of one's sense of self and one's morality, the sense of connectedness to others, and the sense of meaning that one derives from contributing to something larger than oneself (Berman 1997). Young people are continually negotiating a sense of meaning, place, and commitment. In subtle and internal ways they ask, Are there larger purposes that my actions can serve? Do I have a meaningful place in the social and political world? Are there values that I can make a commitment to and people I can stand with? Am I capable of contributing something useful to others and will they welcome and appreciate it? Will my efforts actually make a difference? Do I have the courage to act without guarantees of success? A sense of being connected to one's morality and to the world at large emerges over time and through ongoing dialogue with others.

Throughout childhood and adolescence, young people are formulating a theory of how society works and negotiating their relationship with it. This relationship often remains implicit, visible only in offhand comments expressing their attitudes and judgments about the world around them. Children, in essence, feel their way into the world. The degree of connectedness that they experience determines their interest and participation. In spite of the stereotype that they are egocentric, children care about the welfare of others and about issues of fairness on both a personal and social level. Social responsibility is not a set of behaviors we need to instill in young people but rather behaviors we need to recognize emerging in them.

Children begin constructing their relationship with the political world early in life. The most effective means of helping students develop this relationship is to give them the opportunity to enter and engage the real world around them. Encouraging civic responsibility in young people means connecting them with their community, providing them with the basic social skills to negotiate their differences with others, and teaching them they can make a difference. This does not occur as a result of a set of lessons on specific character traits, customs and manners, or civic responsibility. It occurs when we take the issues of care, connection, and civic action seriously and make them core to the culture and curriculum of the school. It occurs when we look deeply into the ways young people see society operating and help them struggle with how they can make a commitment to a larger sense of meaning for their lives. It occurs when we apply what we know about learning in general to civil and civic education—that we learn best by doing rather than by being told. Eight key factors are critical if socially responsible behavior is to be strengthened and celebrated in our schools. They range from encouraging social skills in an individual to creating opportunities as change agents. The first is developing social skills.

Developing Social Skills

Often adult reaction to incivility and challenging behavior in children is to rewrite and tighten the school's behavior codes. The problematic behavior of young people may be a communication to adults that they do not know how to act with compassion, empathy, and sensitivity in reaction to the needs of others or in response to conflict. Too often we make the assumption that young people have developed, or should have developed, basic social skills. We tend to think that this is the parents' rather than the school's responsibility. However, the development of social skills in a society that tends to provide few effective models either in public life or in the media demands that the school play a prominent role. Like competency skills in reading, writing, and mathematics, such social skills as empathy, cooperation, conflict resolution, and perspective taking require direct instruction.

Research on the social development of children has revealed that children's awareness of the social and political world emerges as early as infancy. Empathy may, in fact, be an innate human attribute that is either nurtured or inhibited by the child's environment. Empathy can be developed by helping children become sensitive observers of the feelings of others and helping them understand the causes of these feelings. Norma Haan and her colleagues (1985) found that children could think in profoundly empathic and moral terms. However, their behavior did not reflect this because they lacked the skills to handle moral conflict. Thus, the key to teaching empathy and moral behavior is training and practice in those skills—perspective taking, conflict resolution, cooperation, assertiveness—that enable us to maintain clarity in conflicted and stressful situations. Whether through role playing, analysis of children's literature, or dealing with actual classroom situations, we can help young children begin to understand and appreciate how another may feel and how they may experience a situation differently.

There are many curriculum materials available in this area and numerous programs that schools can adopt. My school district has been using an empathy development and anger management program produced by the Committee for Children entitled Second Step. We supplement this with conflict resolution material from Educators for Social Responsibility. Second Step is a thirty lesson per grade program that begins in kindergarten. It involves students in role plays and discussions that identify the feeling states of those involved and helps students reflect on and practice various ways of appropriately responding to the situations. Second Step includes a parent component as well so that these skills can be supported at home. A recent study of this program funded by the Center for Disease Control and Prevention found that it was successful in decreasing physical and verbal aggression and in increasing prosocial behavior (Grossman et al. 1997). However, such programs as the Educators for Social Responsibility's Resolving Conflicts Creatively Program, the Stone Center of Wellesley College's Social Competency Program, the Developmental Studies Center's Child Development Project, or the Northeast Foundation for Children's Responsive Classroom are all effective avenues for teaching empathy, cooperation, and conflict resolution skills. In these programs, students are given direct instruction in basic social and emotional skills, and the whole school can become involved in creating a caring community that models respectful and empathetic behavior.

A central theme in the teaching of social skills is the importance of taking the perspective of another. A conflict cannot be resolved until you understand the other side's interests and values. It is only then that you can build on mutual interests without compromising each other's values. In fact, to develop a social consciousness means to be able to step out of one's own perspective and to take on the perspectives of others. But even more than that, it means looking at our own perspective from the vantage point of another. It means presenting ourselves to ourselves and being open to reevaluating our opinions and beliefs.

Although taking the perspective of another and developing self-reflection are part of all the social skills programs mentioned above, these abilities are challenging to nurture. They compel us to live with ambiguity and to be continually open to change. Taking the perspective of another and critically examining our own beliefs and positions can be disconcerting, for it opens our beliefs and positions to questions and challenges. However, developing perspective-taking skills does not undermine our ability to hold beliefs or take positions. We can still stand on our beliefs, but take these stands knowing that we must allow for the possibility that we may be wrong. Taking the perspective of another does not mean a lack of criticalness or of ethical standards, but that we can use our humility and openness to evaluate and act in situations of social conflict with compassion and insight.

There are instructional strategies that can help students develop their ability to take another's perspective and to reflect on their own thinking. Role playing and journal writing are two. At an elementary level it may be simply introducing that there are different perspectives, that some people think one way and that others think another. Martin Hoffman's (1991) inductive discipline—directing a child's attention to the feelings of another—is another strategy. At the secondary level, Educators for Social Responsibility has developed an exercise called methodological belief, which asks students to go beyond comprehending a perspective to fully entering the perspective so that they may find some truth in it. It is only after entering the perspective that they then critique it for its inadequacies and flaws. After doing this exercise in class over a semester one student wrote that he had learned to be less dogmatic about his ideas, more open to change and others' opinions.

Perspective taking not only enables people to be more open to the perceptions of others and more effective at resolving conflicts, it allows people to move away from debate as a mode of discourse toward dialogue. While debate challenges the other position in an effort to demonstrate superiority, dialogue attempts to find common ground among competing positions. Perspective taking and the resulting dialogue are vital to the effective handling of social, moral, and political conflicts as well as to the social, moral, and political development of young people.

Developing a Relationship with Society

Each of us develops a relationship to society and to the world. Furthermore, the way we give meaning to this relationship determines the nature of our participation in the world. I've deliberately chosen the term *relationship* because, like a relationship with another person, our relationship with society includes such powerful factors as interconnection, emotion, influence, and vulnerability.

I use the term relationship because it shifts the context of our thinking. Too often we focus our attention on individual choice and individual responsibility. Most moral education and moral development theory seems directed at the way people make choices, at the way they balance their individual needs with the needs of others. There isn't much attention paid to the social context for these moral decisions. I've found that people don't make moral decisions in isolation, especially not decisions that relate to larger social and political issues. These decisions emerge directly from people's relationship to society—from what they see as the dominant morality in the political culture, and from their sense of their personal ability to influence that culture.

Because it is difficult for many people to describe verbally their relationship to society, I've explored another approach. I've asked people first to draw the way they see their relationship to society. I've collected such pencil, crayon, or marking pen drawings from elementary, high school, and college students, and from adults who represent a wide range of lifestyles and viewpoints. These drawings usually reveal complex feelings toward society—sometimes a rich mosaic of interconnectedness, sometimes the painful expression of alienation and powerlessness, and sometimes the struggle to reconcile both hope and pain. Although we all exist in relationship to society, people seldom talk about the nature of this relationship and how they feel in it. The class of sixth graders, four of whose drawings are reprinted here, were eager to have the opportunity to talk about their joys and frustrations, their hopes and their fears. As the drawings reveal, these children were well aware of the world around them. They saw their relationship to society in very different ways and the dialogue that emerged from these drawings was rich and vital. Young people want to be heard and they want to know how others see things.

From working with these drawings I've realized that helping young people develop a sense of social responsibility means opening a conversation about this relationship. We cannot impose attitudes and

Figure 8–1

Figure 8–2

This is the surroundings in a society, how they affect everyone. At one point in your life you'll probably feel enclosed and surrounded by all these things and they'll really affect you.

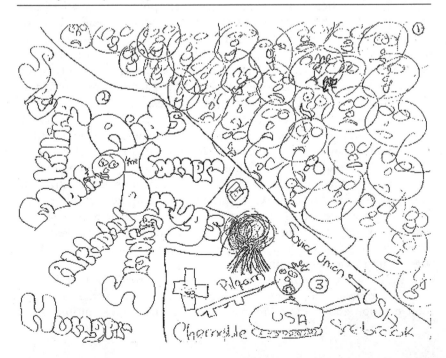

Figure 8–3

Society is just a big blob around me. In my little air bubble there is only my family and friends. I feel different than most of my friends. Maybe it is the way I was brought up, maybe my views on life. I care about the world, but I don't think it concerns me even though it does.

Figure 8–4

understandings. Instead, we must begin a dialogue by listening carefully to young people's ideas and questions. Not only do they need to feel heard and validated in order to grow into meaningful adult roles in society, but we, too, need to learn from them about what their real issues are in order to facilitate their growth most effectively.

Educating for Social Consciousness

Educating for social consciousness means asking: What does the way I lead my life mean for the lives of others? What is my hope for the future? Are my actions consistent with the way I would like the world to be? What can we do together as a community, as a society, and as a world community, that will promote our common good and our common well-being? How can I contribute in a meaningful way to creating a more just, peaceful, and ecologically sound world? Educationally, this means balancing our focus on personal self-realization and personal achievement with an equal focus on social self-realization and collective achievement. When teaching for social responsibility, how we teach and the culture of our classrooms and schools will be of even greater importance than what we teach. We will need to model for students the values and principles of care, justice, empowerment, community, and social responsibility.

Developing a "consciousness of the group" is a skill that can be nurtured, but one that can only be taught experientially. It requires that an individual begins to sense the atmosphere or climate that is present in the group, to observe how people's interactions influence the productivity of the group, and to understand the impact their actions have on the group. Becoming socially responsible means using this consciousness to intervene to improve the group's ability to live and work together. Because the style of instruction in most classrooms is either individualistic or competitive, children do not get the opportunity to develop this skill. Although cooperative learning techniques help, the best way to teach this consciousness is to create classrooms and schools that are functioning communities.

Creating Communities

Community is often used very loosely. When I ask people in workshops to think about a meaningful experience of community in their own lives a rich definition emerges: a community is a group of people who acknowledge their interconnectedness, have a sense of their common purpose, respect their differences, share in group decision making as well as in responsibility for the actions of the group, and support each other's growth. Classrooms and schools can be these kinds of communities but it takes time, intention, and new forms of shared leadership.

Some specific strategies help create community. The first is to have the class or school create a shared set of values or goals that serves as a reminder of their reason for being there. Some teachers have worked with their classes to create a constitution or bills of rights and responsibilities. Others simply have students talk about what rules can help the class function most effectively and how everyone can collaborate to make those rules work.

A second strategy to build community is to encourage students to participate in decision making about the important issues that emerge. These can take the form of class meetings or schoolwide "town meetings," but they need to provide students with the opportunity to share their concerns and to address important issues and conflicts confronting the community. My experience in teaching in and working with democratic schools has taught me that direct democracy is far more effective than representative democracy in creating community. It is in this setting that students experience cooperation, learn how to make good decisions, see the consequences of their actions and decisions, and learn to cope effectively with diversity and conflict.

A third strategy is to pay attention to the group's process and have students collectively evaluate the climate. It is very important to make process observations. Some examples might be: "We haven't functioned well together during the past several days. Are there some reasons for that? Should we be doing some things differently?" or "It seems that people get angry when other people express an opinion that they don't agree with. Is there a way we can listen to them that would communicate more respect for what they have to say?" or "The class sometimes jokes or laughs when someone shares something painful, as if we didn't want to hear it." These reflections teach the class to think about the group as a whole and model for students how to make effective interventions.

Another way to accomplish this is to use checklists or questionnaires that ask students to comment on how the class is doing. Nancy Schniedewind and Ellen Davidson have published two such forms for elementary students (1987). One asks students to evaluate their contributions to the class, the other asks students to think about how well they have listened to others and others have listened to them. Keith Grove, a high school math teacher in Massachusetts, has developed a form he uses in his classes that asks students to describe incidents "where someone helped you understand," "where someone seemed to help another member of the class understand," and "where someone helped our class feel that we are working together." He then asks students to reflect on their own behavior with such questions as: "What do you do that contributes to the success of the class?" "What could you do differently that would help the class have greater success?" and "What do you do, if anything, that hinders the success of the class?" He then allows time for the class to discuss issues that have emerged about how the class is working.

Community cannot exist without conflict. In fact, as M. Scott Peck (1987) points out in his book on community building, the only way to develop a healthy community is through the successful negotiation of conflict. In order to build community in classrooms and schools, we need to teach conflict resolution skills directly and to use the conflicts that naturally emerge as learning opportunities.

Community also cannot exist without affirmation, so finding ways to affirm the members as well as acknowledging the accomplishments is important. In community, people become rich resources to each other. Communities need stories, heroes and heroines, rituals, and celebrations to demonstrate that its members are valued and that people not only care about each other but care about the group as a whole.

Finally, to build community we need to demonstrate new forms of leadership. Leaders—students, teachers, parents, administrators—need to share decision-making power within the group, and trust that the group's collective intelligence is more powerful than any one individual's. They need to know how to facilitate, organize, negotiate, but most of all, listen to the needs and concerns of the various members of the group. And they need to promote others taking leadership as well.

Out of the experience of community young people can become not only conscious of group needs and group process, but they can begin to understand the meaning of the common good, appreciate that they do make a difference to others, and develop a sense of relatedness to the larger human community.

Understanding Our Interdependence

The crises of the last decades—the nuclear threat, destruction of the environment, terrorism, hunger and homelessness on a mass scale, and local and international violence—have demonstrated the smallness of our planet and our inextricable connection with others around the globe. There is no getting "away" anymore. We not only have to understand our interdependence but we need to learn how to get along in an interdependent world.

This is not easy for us. Independence and self-reliance are our dominant national values and inhibit our ability to function in interdependent situations. They are not only pervasive in our political culture but have dominated the "ideology" of child development. This psychological ideology, articulated most clearly by Erikson (1968), holds that the pinnacle of development is autonomy, individuation, and independence—standing on one's own. Gilligan (1982, 1988) and others argue that this construction of development is misleading, that what we have always seen as the adolescent's struggle for autonomy is not a struggle to separate from others, but in fact an attempt to renegotiate their relationship and achieve a position of equality and influence. The adolescent desires connection, affiliation, and involvement but wants to experience their own power, authority, and influence within that connection.

Developing Basic Participatory Understanding and Skills

Social studies programs acquaint students with political institutions and history, yet the age we live in demands a broad and bold set of citizenship skills. We are collectively faced with long-term problems that demand complicated solutions and ongoing attention. Too often, in our hunger for certainty, we grab for simple and inadequate solutions to these complex problems. We fall for slogans of "just say no" and treat symptoms rather than address root causes. Then when these solutions fail, as they must, we blame the victim or the system rather than acknowledge our own short-sightedness. At the same time, politics has become more vicious, confrontational, and oppositional, and interest groups have become more uncompromising. Young people often withdraw from this frustrating and contentious environment. If we are to build a renewed sense of direction and purpose in the United States and encourage young people to enter the political arena, we have to give them the skills to address our most complex problems and to replace the politics of confrontation and opposition with the politics of reconciliation and dialogue.

There are four skills that young people need to learn: *organizing skills* so that they can work well in groups and in organizations to affect change; *consensus-building skills* so that they can transform oppositional debates into productive dialogues; *group problem-solving skills* so that they can draw upon the diverse resources and talents in a group to come up with constructive solutions to complex problems; and *long-term thinking skills* so that they can evaluate the impact that potential solutions may have upon future generations. These skills will enable young people to feel competent to enter the social and political arena, and they are equally applicable to family, work, and neighborhood issues.

To develop the courage to participate, young people also need the hope given them with examples of individuals and organizations that are making a difference. We need to tell them of the Mahatma Gandhis and the Martin Luther Kings, but also of the people who live down the street who are improving the neighborhood, and the organizations that help individuals make a difference. Putting students in touch with these people and organizations can help them see how deeply people care and how worthwhile it is to participate in creating change.

This kind of education may create political activists. But first it will help young people see that their daily actions are creating the world as it is and as it will be. They can come to understand that we make a difference in our relationships with friends, in our work, in raising children, in our role as consumers, not by the political positions we espouse but by how we live—the consciousness and integrity we bring to our actions and the care we take with others.

Exploring Real World Issues

Children develop an awareness of the social and political world at a very early age and can be passionate about its dangers and potential (Connell 1971; Hess and Torney 1967; Jennings and Niemi 1974; Sigel and Hoskin 1981; Moore, Lare, and Wagner 1985). Moore, Lare, and Wagner found that knowledge of such key organizing concepts as law and how laws are formed, elections and the electoral process, and the role of Congress gave children the conceptual framework from which to integrate additional political knowledge. Children hear a great deal about the political world from current events reported by the media or discussed by their parents. Yet without some way to make these events meaningful, children develop only the most cursory and simplistic understandings of these events and the issues, concerns, and political processes behind them.

Examining social and political issues should not simply be relegated to social studies. Science studies can investigate issues related to the environment and technology. Math studies can examine how numbers are used in our political process to persuade or deceive. English studies can include the literature of social change. Business studies can focus on the larger social and ethical questions raised by business practices. Art studies can study the use of art in creating propaganda or in communicating one's perception of social and political issues. At the elementary level there are appropriate strategies for engaging children in meaningful conversations about social and political issues (write to ESR for Susan Jones' 10 Point Model for Teaching Controversial Issues). Creating a dialogue about real world issues not only increases young people's engagement with the world around them, but enables them to develop skills in handling the ethical dilemmas that these issues pose.

One example of curriculum in this area is a ninth-grade course created by the Hudson (MA) Public Schools. Teachers have developed a core course that integrates English and Civics and whose essential question is: What are the rights and responsibilities of an individual in a just society? The course integrates literature, history, civics, and community service learning into an experience in which students confront important social and political issues. A central part of this course is the Facing History and Ourselves curriculum developed by the Facing History and Ourselves Foundation. This curriculum engages students in the study of the roots of two twentieth-century genocides, the Holocaust and the Armenian genocide, and, by extension, more recent attempted genocides in Cambodia and Bosnia. The curriculum confronts young people with the human potential for passivity, complicity, and destructiveness by asking how genocide can become state policy. It raises significant ethical questions and sensitizes them to injustice, inhumanity, suffering, and the abuse of power. At the same time it is academically challenging and helps complicate students' thinking so that they do not accept simple answers to complex problems. Students confront their own potential for passivity and complicity, their own prejudices and intolerances, and their own moral commitments. The curriculum develops students' perspective-taking and social-reasoning abilities and students emerge with a greater sense of moral responsibility and a greater commitment to participate in making a difference.

Too often instruction in controversial issues simply presents students with the depressing evidence of the problems we face. This often leads to despair rather than empowerment as students realize they have no solutions. We need to give students opportunities for involvement and action. We need to present multiple perspectives on problems, as well as teach how conflict resolution strategies can be applied to depolarize the conflict and promote dialogue.

Most of all, we need to follow students' thinking. Bettelheim points out that "the reason for the higher academic achievement of Japanese youngsters may well be that the Japanese child . . . is invited to think things out on his own, a habit that stands him in good stead when he has to master academic material. The American child, in contrast, is expected to conform his decisions and actions to what he is told to do. This expectation certainly does not encourage him to do his own thinking" (Bettelheim 1985, 58). A second-grade teacher taught me to begin each unit by asking students three questions—What do you know about this? What do you think you know but are not sure about? and What questions do you have?—and structure the unit around the questions the students indicated were most pressing for them. Teaching this way not only helped me understand my students better but developed in them a respect for their knowledge, their thinking ability, and their power to guide their learning (Berman and LaFarge 1993).

Opportunities for Social Contribution

Social understanding and social responsibility are built on children's desire to understand and feel effective in the social world, to initiate and maintain connection with others, and to reach out to those in distress. Therefore, the final step in nurturing social consciousness and social responsibility must be encouraging students to participate in the world. What children do to serve the community matters less than whether it is something they see as important and something they choose. The opportunities and designs are endless. The key is encouraging students to instigate and develop community service learning experiences marked by continuity, depth, and meaningfulness that encourage an ethic of care and an ethic of service throughout their school years.

The research shows that those who are active early in life, whether in school or the community, are more likely to be active later in life. The studies of programs involving students in active engagement in the social and political arena indicate that this involvement may be an important stepping stone to later participation (Berman 1997). We tend to treat young people as "citizens-in-preparation" rather than active members of their community, and give them little responsibility for acting on citizenship skills.

Whether it is having students help each other or having students participate in local community efforts, students need instruction and coaching. Young people need to learn how best to help others, how to be patient, and how to tolerate the slow pace of change. They also need to hear about the success stories of others—students who have reclaimed forests, cleaned up rivers, improved their school environment, helped the homeless. Community service learning efforts not only give students the opportunity to contribute and see that they can make a difference, they build self-esteem and allow students to experience themselves as part of the larger network of people who are helping to create a better world.

Conclusion

As teachers, we want our students to reach their fullest potential. We care about them and want them to reach beyond what they see as their limits. Probably there is no better symbol for this than the outdoor adventure programs, outward bound programs, and ropes courses that have become a basic part of the more progressive physical education programs. These programs challenge us to go beyond our fears and our limits to see our potential for courage and accomplishment. Yet the real ropes course is participating in our social and political system. If we focus our attention on this ropes course, we can help our students see their potential for courage and accomplishment in helping to create a more just, peaceful, and ecologically sound world.

Works Cited

Berman, S. 1997. *Children's Social Consciousness and the Development of Social Responsibility.* Albany, NY: SUNY Press.

Berman, S., and P. LaFarge. 1993. *Promising Practices in Teaching Social Responsibility.* Albany, NY: SUNY Press.

Bettelheim, B. 1985. "Punishment Versus Discipline." *Atlantic* 256: 51–59.

Connell, R. W. 1971. *The Child's Construction of Politics.* Melbourne, Australia: Melbourne University Press.

Erikson, E. 1968. *Identity: Youth and Crisis.* New York: W.W. Norton.

Gilligan, C. 1988. "Adolescent Development Reconsidered." In *Mapping the Moral Domain,* by C. Gilligan, J. V. Ward, J. M. Taylor, and B. Bardige. Cambridge, MA: Harvard University Press.

————. 1982. *In a Different Voice.* Cambridge: Harvard University Press.

Grossman, D. C., H. J. Neckerman, T. D. Koepsell, P. Y. Liu, K. N. Asher, K. Beland, K. S. Frey, and F. P. Rivara. 1997. "Effectiveness of a Violence Prevention Curriculum Among Children in Elementary School." *Journal of the American Medical Association* 277:1605–11.

Haan, N., E. Aerts, and B. Cooper. 1985. *On Moral Grounds: The Search for Practical Morality.* New York: New York University Press.

Hess, R., and J. Torney. 1967. *The Development of Political Attitudes in Children.* Chicago: Aldine Publishing.

Hoffman, M. L. 1991. "Empathy, Social Cognition, and Moral Action." In *Handbook of Moral Behavior and Development, Volume 1: Theory,* edited by W. Kurtines and J. Gewirtz. Hillsdale, NJ: Lawrence Erlbaum.

————. 1984. "Empathy, Its Limitations, and Its Role in a Comprehensive Moral Theory." In *Morality, Moral Behavior, and Moral Development,* edited by W. Kurtines and J. Gewirtz. New York: Wiley.

Jennings, M. K., and R. G. Nemi. 1974. *The Political Character of Adolescents.* Princeton, NJ: Princeton University Press.

Keniston, K. 1968. *The Young Radicals: Notes on Committed Youth.* New York: Harcourt, Brace and World.

————. 1960. *The Uncommitted: Alienated Youth in American Society.* New York: Harcourt, Brace and World.

Moore, S. W., J. Lare, and K. A. Wagner. 1985. *The Child's Political Worlds: A Longitudinal Perspective.* New York: Praeger.

Peck, M. S. 1987. *A Different Drum.* New York: Simon and Schuster.

Schniedewind, N., and E. Davidson. 1987. *Cooperative Learning, Cooperative Lives.* Dubuque, IA: Wm. C. Brown.

Sigel, R. S., and M. B. Hoskin. 1981. *The Political Involvement of Adolescents.* New Brunswick, NJ: Rutgers University Press.

Calling Students to Action:
How Wayland Middle School Puts a Curriculum
for Social Responsibility into Practice

Stephen Feinberg, Richard Schaye,
and David Summergrad

Stephen is the Social Studies Curriculum Leader at Wayland Middle School where he has been teaching for eighteen years. Richard has been the principal of Wayland Middle School for fifteen years. David has taught at Wayland Middle School for twenty-three years and is presently the English Curriculum Leader and the Houseleader for Martin Luther King House.

At Wayland Middle School, in Wayland, Massachusetts, the curriculum and the structure of the school combine to support the students' basic drive to be part of things. Sheldon Berman tells us, "Helping students develop a sense of social responsibility also means directly and intentionally nurturing in them a positive and empowered relationship with society." To do that effectively, our school provides a powerful, thoughtful curriculum centered around two essential ingredients, caring and justice, which build the bridges between students and the communities around them.

Berman challenged us to "take the issues of care, connection, and civic action seriously and make them core to the culture and curriculum of the school." In 1984, our principal, Richard Schaye, decided to rename each of the grades in the school. He selected names of three American heroes whose lives demonstrated that individuals can become meaningful contributing citizens through their actions. The sixth grade became the Henry David Thoreau House. Using the unique individualistic approach of this famous writer, issues of personal conscience and respect for the serenity and beauty of our local environment were folded into the existing curriculum. The seventh grade was called the Rachel Carson House, where environmental issues became the focus. And the eighth grade was named the Martin Luther King House, where the study of social equity issues and racism began to be interwoven with existing courses. Concentrating on these individuals and the related themes over the three-year middle school period served as a wake-up call for civic responsibility.

We have developed courses of studies and specific activities around these themes along with many opportunities for individual and group action related to them. Parental support for this approach has been remarkably positive. As one parent put it, "Our dinner time is no longer the inevitable discussion of what do you have for homework tonight. That question now shares time with what we as a family can do about the environment or why full equality is so difficult to achieve. It has helped us see our children as future adults."

Students in the sixth grade are involved in activities like the "Making a Difference" projects, which involve students in activities ranging from collecting food for homeless shelters to gathering pet supplies for a local veterinary hospital. As members of the school recycling crew in the seventh grade, the students take more responsibility for both collecting items for reuse and cleaning the environment in and around the school. As students develop their sense of wonder, they also develop a sense of concern. "What can I do about the environment?" is a question seventh graders ask. This individual worry soon broadens into the realization of a need for collective action, and students begin to ask: "What can we do?"

Eighth graders explore the social studies curriculum, building on their understanding of environmental issues, as a way to think about injustice in the world today. Dr. King told us, "Injustice anywhere is a threat to justice everywhere." Students write letters to leaders, celebrities, and policy makers as they try to make sense of a world where inequality and unfairness abound. Each time the students receive a response it not only increases their knowledge, but it reinforces their belief that their voices are heard—that individual action matters! Students use these exchanges to broaden the definition of the boundaries of their own community. They begin to realize that they exist in a larger community beyond the town of Wayland.

We have no illusions that our house structure is a panacea. Students still call each other names, leave gum under the tables, and stare awkwardly at each other at dances. Nor would it be accurate to imply that these three heroes—Thoreau, Carson, and King—and their ideas infuse all that we do in our school. Much of the daily routine is similar to most middle schools across America. What is distinctive is that we use these three themes to continually and consciously make connections between in-school study and out-of-school problem solving. Where many schools have embraced the notion of service, few have tied that spirit of service to the core curriculum and themes in the manner Berman suggests. Our "ropes course" is a three-year progression that develops social consciousness through a combination of curriculum and social action.

We have biked together in the spirit of Henry David Thoreau; we have collected trash from the woods in the spirit of Rachel Carson; and we have confronted racial injustice bolstered by the courage of Dr. King. The models of Thoreau, Carson, and King have set our students on the course to responsible citizenship. They have learned that as true citizens in a participatory democracy they need not be afraid to take individual actions or to develop and express their own beliefs.

In the words of one juror in Reginald Rose's classic courtroom drama *Twelve Angry Men* (a play read by all our seventh graders): "It takes a great deal of courage to stand alone." It is our hope that on our best days the ethos of Wayland Middle School helps each of our students respond with a little more courage.

Afterword

Teachers Committed to the Struggle for Democracy: Cuesta lo que Cuesta

Peter McLaren

Living under the sway of capitalist expansionism, corporate globalism, the destructive effects of consumer culture, and the juggernaut of imperial market forces, it is impossible to lose sight of the withering condition of democracy and the triumph of neoliberalism. Hypostatizing accumulation above an ethics of democracy, contemporary incarnations of capitalist fundamentalism threaten to sever the arteries of whatever remains of the public sphere. Living in this historical juncture has strengthened my commitment and reaffirmed my resolve to realign critical pedagogy with liberatory politics, whose unembarrassed modus vivendi is anticapitalist struggle.

Several times Paulo Freire conveyed to me his profound concern that critical pedagogy no longer concerned itself very much with larger global issues such as hierarchical division of international labor and was in danger of being domesticated and denuded of its emancipatory politics. Capitalist exploitation functioned as an axiomatic given, as received common sense. Freire worried that in time critical pedagogy would simply become a toolbox for creating what some critics have called "boutique" forms of democratic classroom arrangements, display windows that reflect the superficial forms of democratic classrooms—discussion circles, student-centered curricula, teachers serving as "facilitators," and so on. Yet such pedagogical fashion shows would be devoid of substantive social critique. The reenchantment of critical pedagogy must take teachers and students away from what I have called "the democracy of empty forms" in order to engage in conversations with the fullness of history and the lives and teachings of men and women who struggled over what forms history takes. Malcolm X, Che Guevara, Camillo Torres, Ricardo Flores Magon, Rosa Luxemburg, and Rosa Parks are just a few voices from the past that should figure prominently in a revisioning of the practice of pedagogy so that it can consist of broader efforts at building a more humane and just social order.

While it is necessary that we create conditions for active learning, for codeveloping courses with students, for the co-construction of classroom knowledge, for building a community of learners, for creating the contexts for connection, affiliation, and involvement, for the creation of critical self-reflexivity, and for developing learner-centered rhythms in our pedagogical practices, we need to keep focused peda-gogically on the objective fact of what Karl Marx called *the working day* and the changing relations of production under global capitalism. The working day is what defines our needs, our aspirations, our daily struggle. Clearly, the objective conditions surrounding the working day are swiftly changing in the wake of global economic restructuring. The opportunities for economic survival and freedom from necessity are growing ever more dim. As educators we ask ourselves: How do we teach our students about the present conditions that await them? What should we say about the increase in low-wage, part-time work; the dis-appearance of middle and upper level managerial jobs that were for generations the stuff of the American Dream; dwindling unemploy-ment benefits; the growth of anti-union sentiment and the ugly likeli-hood of permanent structural unemployment?

The fear that sits in waiting, ready to convulse our students, is not that young adults will lose their livelihood but that they will never have the opportunity to have a livelihood. It is not only the poor that have lost out on the American Dream, but the vast majority of Americans. In the face of this daunting scenario, is it enough for progressive educators to encourage their students to become more "postmodern" social actors, to break established codes of convention, to find their own "voice," to march to their own drummer, or to disrupt normalized social practices? Such acts of transgression rarely stem from critical consciousness or a deep understanding of the social contradictions tied to the laws of motion of capital that profoundly shape the contours of our social world. Further, such acts of avant-garde activism often follow in the wake of the trajectory of affluent desire. What's missing from critical pedagogy in these most postmodern of times—a concern shared by many authors in this book—is precisely an effort to create the class-room conditions that will help *explain* the contradictions of everyday life as they are manifested in the daily lives of our students, in their lived relationship to the domain of the social. For instance, how are the "desires" of students and teachers experienced on a daily basis so that they are understood as disconnected from the poverty of other neigh-borhoods or the structured inequality experienced by other countries? How are sexism, racism, and class exploitation produced and shaped by the social relations of late capitalism? Raising such uncomfortable questions recognizes that pedagogy is always a historical set of prac-tices, that it is forever insinuated in class, ethnic, and gender antago-nisms. A pedagogy devoid of critique allows relations of exploitation to go unannounced and when such a condition remains uninterrupted, it can only rehabilitate the fundamental lie of capital. Such a scenario cre-ates the conditions for personal desires to be misidentified as universal needs delinked from capitalist social relations. Critical educators need to analyze the linkages between students and their desires and the steady diet of narratives of citizenship that are offered to the population through classroom rituals and routines, through informational networks, through broadcast media. A critique of global capitalism and its relationship to patriarchy, homophobia, and racism is fundamental to a transformative politics of classroom democracy. Social critique must become the cornerstone of a critical pedagogy for the new millennium.

Such a pedagogy stipulates the creation of knowledge practices in our classrooms that are able to contest ways of knowing and living that repress multiplicity and difference. In order to achieve such pedagogical conditions, critical educators need to ask different sets of questions: In what ways might our practices of creating democratic classrooms reconfirm, reinitiate, or reposition our students more securely in relations of domination and subordination, despite our best intentions? In what ways is our pedagogical self-fashioning unintentionally complicitous in reinscribing dominant social relations linked to established race, class, and gender hierarchies? We need to confront such questions as uncomfortable as they might make us feel. As critical educators, we must refuse to confine our inquiry to the internal dynamics of classroom organization; rather, we must recognize that in many instances the contradictions characteristic of our pedagogical practices reflect many of the social contradictions of the wider society.

Due to the reconversion of the global economy to a neoliberal assault on the poor and the transformation of the globe into a giant *malquiladora* industrial park, diasporic movements of ethnic groups across national borders have transformed classrooms into intercultural arenas, sites of heterotopic forms of everyday life, a *transfrontera* terrain where many cultures make contact and sometimes collide. As a result of this cultural smudging of codes, we can begin to redefine the meaning of United States citizenship and national identity. The uneven power relationships within the dominant Anglocentric culture are now being unmasked and challenged by educators employing a critical border pedagogy. Whereas mainstream pedagogy too often engages students in the cruel theatre of assimilation, critical border educators are decentering Anglocentrism and redrawing the map of citizenship and identity from various perspectives and standpoint epistemologies. In such a climate students need to build democratic communities in classrooms so that the Anglo-imperial backlash against immigration, bilingual education, and multiculturalism, bolstered by a growing Latinophobia, can be stemmed by the furious solidarity of collective struggle.

Beyond the Silence: Listening for Democracy shifts our pedagogical center of gravity toward the quest for democracy and social justice. When a sixth-grade class develops a language arts unit in order to pro-

duce literature on safety for their age group after the abduction and
murder of one of their peers, when a fifth-grade class decides to
explore Asiatic heritages through a study of Angel Island (the immi-
grant processing center through which many of their ancestors had
passed), and when second graders produce a regularly broadcast radio
show in order to learn language arts skills, then students have made the
necessary break from mainstream "banking" approaches to education,
criticized by Paulo Freire, and are beginning to take the necessary steps
to create the conditions for democratic learning.

   Beyond the Silence points toward the creation of pedagogical relations that foster hope in a world given over to the madness of capitalist consumerism and commodification. And here I use the term *hope*
not in an idealized or abstract sense but rather with the recognition that
unless hope is conjugated with struggle and brought within the orbit of
radical love, it remains an ephemeral thought, cleansed of conviction,
floating insouciantly outside the entrance to human history.

   This wonderful volume speaks to the promise of a democracy that
we can hear rustling in the autumn leaves, a democracy struggling to
be heard, one whose cry is as yet too faint to be recognized above the
babble of politicians and education officials. The promise of democracy grows stronger the more that we are willing to acknowledge its
constitutive failure to serve the interests of more than a small portion
of the population. Democracy is still only a dream, but one that is
worth following. The teachers and students in this volume are struggling to achieve such a dream. Let's listen to their stories of hope.

Work Cited

Marx, Karl. 1997. *Capital: A Critique of Political Economy.* Vol. 1. Translated
   by B. Fowkes. New York: Vintage.

*Peter McLaren is a professor of education at the University of
California, Los Angeles, and author/editor of numerous works
on critical pedagogy.*

Resources

Association for Experiential Education
(publishers of *The Journal of Experiential Education*)
2305 Canyon Blvd., Suite 100
Boulder, CO 80302

Center for Democratic Living
Frankie Moore Lappé and Paul DuBois
289 Fox Farm Road
P.O. Box 818
Brattleboro, VT 05301
(802) 254–1234

Collaborative for the Advancement of Social and Emotional Learning
(CASEL)
Department of Psychology (M/C 285)
University of Illinois at Chicago
1007 W. Harrison Street
Chicago, IL 60607–7137
(312) 413–1008

Committee for Children (Second Step)
2203 Airport Way South, Suite 5000
Seattle, WA 98134
(800) 634–4449

Compact for Learning and Citizenship
Education Commission of the States
707 17th Street, Suite 2700
Denver, CO 80202–3427
(303) 299–3629

Developmental Studies Center
2000 Embarcadero, Suite 305
Oakland, CA 94606
(800) 666–7270

Dewey Society (publishers of *Educational Theory*)
University of Illinois College of Education
1310 S. Sixth Street
Champaign, IL 61820

Educators for Social Responsibility
23 Garden Street
Cambridge, MA 02138
(800) 370–2515

Encounter: Educating for Meaning and Social Justice (formerly *Holistic Education Review*)
P.O. Box 328
Brandon, VT 05733

Facing History and Ourselves Foundation
16 Hurd Road
Brookline, MA 02146
(617) 232–6919

The Foxfire Fund, Inc. (publisher of *The Active Learner,* formerly *Hands On*)
P.O. Box 541
Mountain City, GA 30562
(706) 746–5828

Free Sprit Publishing Inc.
400 First Avenue North, Suite 616
Minneapolis, MN 55401–1724
(800) 735–7323

Highlander Research and Education Center
1959 Highlander Way
New Market, TN 37820
(423) 933–3443

Institute for Democracy in Education (publisher of the journal *Democracy and Education*)
313 McCracken Hall
College of Education
Ohio University
Athens, OH 45701–2979

Institute for Global Communications
Presidio Building 1012, First Floor
Torney Avenue
P.O. Box 29904
San Francisco, CA 94129–0904

LeARN (Learning Alternatives Resource Network)
Orange County Department of Education
200 Kalmus Dr. Box 9050
Costa Mesa, CA 92628
(714) 966–4490

Network of Educators on the Americas (NECA)
P.O. Box 73038
Washington, DC 20056–3038
(202) 238–2379

Northeast Foundation for Children
71 Montague City Road
Greenfield, MA 01301
(800) 360–6332

Progressive Educator
http:/www.newmaine.com/progressive-educator/

Resource Center for Redesigning Education
P.O. Box 1069
Williston, VT 05495

Rethinking Schools (publisher of *Rethinking Schools*)
1001 East Keefe Avenue
Milwaukee, WI 53212

Southern Poverty Law Center (publisher of *Teaching Tolerance*)
400 Washington Ave.
Montgomery, AL 36104

The Stone Center
Wellesley College
106 Central Street
Wellesley, MA 02181–8268
(781) 283–2847

William Glasser Institute
22024 Lassen Street, Suite 118
Chatsworth, CA 91311–3600
(818) 700–8000

Annotated Bibliography

These are books that the contributors have found helpful in their research for democratic teaching. Some are old classics, some brand-new. They are offered as suggestions for further reading.

Apple, M. 1993. *Official Knowledge: Democratic Education in a Conservative Age.* New York: Routledge.
   Critiques current trends toward the commercialization and privatization of schools, and presents efforts to create democratic education.

Berman, S., and P. LaFarge, eds. 1993. *Promising Practices in Teaching Social Responsibility.* Albany: SUNY Press.
   A collection of essays discussing classroom practices to create social responsibility.

Berman, S. 1997. *Children's Social Consciousness and the Development of Social Responsibility.* Albany: SUNY Press.
   This book shares the years of research Berman has collected about how children become socially responsible.

Beyer, L., ed. 1996. *Creating Democratic Classrooms: The Struggle to Integrate Theory and Practice.* New York: Teachers College Press.
   A collection of essays that describe the actions of teachers attempting to teach democratically.

Cummins, J., and D. Sayers. 1997. *Brave New Schools: Challenging Cultural Illiteracy Through Global Learning Networks.* New York: St. Martin's Griffin.
   Both a critique and a comprehensive reference that presents hundreds of Internet resources.

Dennison, G. 1969. *The Lives of Children: A Practical Description of Freedom in Its Relation to Growth and Learning.* New York: Random House.
   This is the story of a pioneering experiment in running a free school in New York's East Side and is filled with practical ideas for teachers who want to make their classrooms and schools more democratic and productive.

Developmental Studies Center. 1994. *At Home in Our Schools.* Oakland, CA: DSC.
   A guide to schoolwide activities that build community. Includes ideas from the Child Development Project for parents, teachers, and administrators.

Dewey, J. 1916. *Democracy in Education.* New York: Macmillan.
   Arguably the father of progressive education. This slender volume houses Dewey's famous essay on what elements create a democratic education.

———. 1990. *The School and Society. The Child and the Curriculum.* Chicago: University of Chicago.
   Presents Dewey's radical philosophy of education as experimental and child-centered.

Fraser, J. 1997. *Reading, Writing, and Justice: School Reform as if Democracy Matters*. Albany: SUNY Press.
The author poses and answers this question: What would it mean to take democracy seriously in today's debate about school reform?

Freire, P. 1995. *Pedagogy of the Oppressed*. New York: Continuum.
This book is Freire's most popular. It discusses the transformative effect literacy can have on the poor and unrepresented, drawing from his years of experience as an educator and activist.

Gardner, H. 1985. *Frames of Mind: The Theory of Multiple Intelligences*. New York: Basic Books.
This book forwards the theory that there are many ways to measure success, IQ being only one, and does so with exhaustive scientific and anecdotal support.

Gilligan, C. 1982. *In a Different Voice: Psychological Theory and Women's Development*. Cambridge, MA: Harvard University Press.
A feminist perspective about a moral continuum and its effect on our perception of women.

Giroux, H. A., C. Lankshea, P. McLaren, and M. Peters. 1996. *Counternarratives: Cultural Studies and Critical Pedagogies in Postmodern Spaces*. New York: Routledge.
The chapters apply a strong critical application of postmodern theory to cultural studies and education in exploring the media, technology, and schooling within our everyday human struggles.

Glasser, W. 1998. *Choice Theory*. New York: HarperCollins.
William Glasser's latest contribution to education, in which he clearly describes "choice theory" as a grounding for the psychological understanding of behavior. All of his books are highly recommended.

Goleman, D. 1995. *Emotional Intelligence*. New York: Bantam Books.
This book complements anyone's assumptions about intelligence with scientific, anecdotal, and philosophical support that challenge the reader to redefine intelligence and its potential.

Gordon, T. 1974. *Teacher Effectiveness Training: T.E.T.* New York: Peter H. Wyden.
How to instill a sense of intrinsic motivation and discipline for quality work and behavior is a major concern of every teacher, and Gordon offers practical, how-to advice highlighted by numerous examples here. All of his books are recommended.

Gutman, A. 1994. *Democratic Education*. New York: Routledge.
This book deals with our attempts to secure the ideals of democracy within the American educational institution while avoiding jargon and labels.

Hern, M., ed. 1996. *Deschooling Our Lives*. Philadelphia: New Society.
This collection of easy-to-read essays offers an overview of what many different types of alternative ways of educating children can look like, from free schools to home schooling.

Herndon, J. 1969. *The Way It's 'Spozed to Be*. New York: Bantam Books.
A serious, sad, and humorous account of life in a ghetto school, this book shows how all involved, except the children, seem to conspire to uneducate.

———. 1971. *How to Survive in Your Native Land*. New York: Simon & Schuster.
Highly recommended, this classic describes with unusual wit and insight the subtleties of a middle class suburban junior high and how it systematically destroys children's spirits.

Holt, J. 1970. *What Do I Do Monday?* New York: E.P. Dutton & Co.
Filled with practical ideas and suggestions for teachers interested in making their classrooms more relevant and interesting, changes our schools desperately need today.

hooks, b. 1994. *Teaching to Transgress: Education as the Practice of Freedom*. New York: Routledge.
hooks raises important critical questions about power and boundaries and defines education: "the practice of freedom is a way of teaching that anyone can learn."

Horton, M. 1997. *The Long Haul*. New York: Teachers College Press.
The autobiography of Myles Horton, innovator, collaborator, teacher, and rebel.

Horton, M., and P. Freire. 1990. *We Make the Road by Walking: Conversations on Education and Social Change*. Philadelphia: Temple University Press.
A "talking book" by two great teacher-activists of the late twentieth century, who discuss the role of education.

Humes, E. 1996. *No Matter How Loud I Shout: A Year in the Life of Juvenile Court*. New York: Simon & Schuster.
A well-researched book about life within the juvenile justice system.

Isaac, K. 1992. *Civics for Democracy: A Journey for Teachers and Students*. Washington, DC: Essential Books.
A textbooklike compilation that includes resources, ideas for activism, and encouragement.

Knapp, C. 1992. *Lasting Lessons: A Teacher's Guide to Reflecting on Experience*. Charleston, WV: ERIC.
Necessary reading for every teacher interested in the theoretical and practical art and science of reflection.

———. 1996. *Just Beyond the Classroom: Community Adventures for Interdisciplinary Learning*. Charleston, WV: ERIC.
Continues Knapp's search for connection between collaborative learning and reflection.

Kohl, H. 1991. *I Won't Learn from You: And Other Thoughts on Creative Maladjustment*. New York: New Press.
This collection of thought-provoking essays centers around being educated from the students' point of view and gives voice to those whose views of the world don't match the lockstep expectations of mass education.

———. 1967. *36 Children*. New York: Penguin Books.
This tale of Kohl as a young teacher in a Harlem sixth-grade class offers creative solutions and an uncanny insight into the possibilities of teaching with the kids.

Kohn, A. 1986. *No Contest: The Case Against Competition: Why We Lose in Our Race to Win*. Boston: Houghton Mifflin.
This book challenges our most taken-for-granted assumptions about how we operate in the world and why fostering competition undermines our achievement for success.

————. 1990. *The Brighter Side of Human Nature: Altruism and Empathy in Everyday Life*. Boston: Houghton Mifflin.
An analysis of our basic abilities at being empathetic.

————. 1993. *Punished by Rewards: The Trouble with Gold Stars, Incentive Plans, A's, Praise, and Other Bribes*. Boston: Houghton Mifflin.
A comprehensive view of behaviorism and its negative effects on building trusting and democratic schools.

————. 1996. *Beyond Discipline: From Compliance to Community*. Alexandria, VA: ASCD Publications.
This book describes useful ways to rethink discipline.

Lakes, R. 1996. *Youth Development and Critical Education: The Promise of Democratic Action*. Albany: SUNY Press.
Documents grassroots efforts by youth.

Lappé, F. M. 1989. *Rediscovering America's Values*. New York: Ballantine Books.
When Frankie went on a search for examples of grassroots democratic action, she created this book.

Leonard, G. 1991. *Mastery: The Keys to Long-Term Success and Fulfillment*. New York: Dutton.
A longtime practitioner of the martial arts, Leonard makes a convincing argument about the need for practice to reach quality.

Llewellyn, G. 1991. *The Teenage Liberation Handbook: How to Quit School and Get a Real Life Education*. Washington, DC: Essential Books.
Written by a former middle school teacher, this unique account validates the view of many kids that school is irrelevant and then challenges them to create productive, meaningful experiences for themselves.

McLaren, P. 1989. *Life in Schools: An Introduction to Critical Pedagogy in the Foundations of Education*. New York: Longman.
This book answers the flip side to what is working in our schools by comprehensively documenting what has gone and continues to go on in the undermining of education.

Neill, A. S. 1961. *Summerhill*. New York: Hart.
Summerhill, the pioneering school in England that is today run by Neill's daughter, operates on both the principles of true democracy and the elements of a therapeutic community. This book is well written, easy to read, and offers a comprehensive overview of the Free School.

————. 1961. *Freedom: Not License*. New York: Hart.
A sequel to Summerhill *and an expansion of Neill's philosophy, this is an excellent book for those not only interested in instilling intrinsic motivation and self-discipline in children, but also understanding the fine line between democratic and autocratic practice.*

Novak, J. M., ed. 1994. *Democratic Teacher Education: Programs, Processes, Problems, and Prospects*. Albany: SUNY Press.
A collection of essays by mostly higher education folks who are working to create democratic practice.

Paley, V. G. 1992. *You Can't Say You Can't Play*. Cambridge, MA: Harvard University Press.
This firsthand account of a kindergarten teacher explores the moral dimensions of the classroom.

Peck, M. S. 1987. *The Different Drum: Community Making and Peace.* New York: Simon & Schuster.
A book that defines the developmental nature of community.

Postman, N., and C. Weingartner. 1969. *Teaching as a Subversive Activity.* New York: Delacorte.
A piercing analysis of the sickness of our schools based as they often are on fear, coercion, and ritual learning, this title suggests alternative ways to bring meaning into your classroom.

Rogers, C. 1969. *Freedom to Learn.* Columbus, OH: Merrill.
A basic philosophic statement about learning as a process, Rogers draws from his years of experience in the field of psychology and human growth including a few chapters by teachers and colleagues to discuss how schools can choose to enhance this idea of education as a process.

Rohnke, K. 1984. *Silver Bullets: A Guide to Initiative Problems, Adventure Games, and Trust Activities.* Hamilton, MA: Project Adventure, Inc.
A must-read for teachers who want to build the sense of community in their classroom tomorrow, this book offers a plethora of games aimed at instigating the practice of teamwork, cooperation, and redefining the class atmosphere.

Rose, M. 1989. *Lives on the Boundary: A Moving Account of the Struggles and Achievements of America's Educationally Underprepared.* New York: Penguin.
Rose works with underprepared adults and children with unique methods that challenge readers to question their assumptions about how we teach, student potential, and democratic practice.

Silberman, C. 1970. *Crisis in the Classroom.* New York: Random House.
Required reading for all concerned about education, this book not only documents how schools are harming children, but also provides some promising ideas on how our schools can be changed with rich, vivid, real-life examples.

Sizer, T. R. 1996. *Horace's Hope: What Works for the American High School.* Boston: Houghton Mifflin.
With a fictional principal narrating, Sizer illuminates with insight and many candid stories the myriad problems, choices, and ideas schools across America face today.

Wood, G. H. 1992. *Schools That Work: America's Most Innovative Public Education Programs.* New York: Dutton.
Wood has taken a journey across America and written this book to inspire us to improve education with suggestions on where we can start.